SPEAKING FRANKLY

What Makes a Woman Good In Bed

Wendy Leigh

FREDERICK MULLER LIMITED
LONDON

First published in Great Britain 1978 by
Frederick Muller Limited, London, NW2 6LE

ISBN: 0 584 10342 5

British Library Cataloguing in Publication Data

Leigh, Wendy
    Speaking frankly.
    1. Sex
    I. Title
    301.41'7   HQ21

    ISBN 0—584—10342—5

Typeset by Texet, Boreham Wood, Herts and
Printed and bound in Great Britain by
Redwood Burn Limited
Trowbridge and Esher

This book is for the memory of Maria, my influence, wishing she could have read it. For my 'adopted' sister, Jane Lovelle. For my mother, Marion. With my love and admiration.

Contents

Acknowledgements   ix

Introduction   1

The Sexperts   17
Sex Therapist   19
Feminist   24
Psychologist   25
Dr. Martin Cole   29
Xaviera Hollander   34
Call Girl   38
Pimp   41
Male Prostitute   44

'Swinging Sixties'   47
Mandy Rice Davies   49
Jack Nicholson   51
Justin de Villeneuve   51
Michael Caine   54
Vicki Hodge   54
Bernie Cornfeld   57
Patrick Lichfield   57
John Wayne   62
Imogen Hassall   63
Germaine Greer   66

The Music World   69
Eartha Kitt   71
Tony Bennett   73
Isaac Hayes   73
Engelbert Humperdinck   77
Roger Daltrey   78
Sonny Bono   81
Barry White   81
Debbie Reynolds   84

The Music World (continued)
Bianca Jagger   84
Gladys Knight   90
Angie Bowie   90
Susan George   93

Media Men and Women   95
Michael Parkinson   97
Hugh Hefner   99
Jilly Cooper   100
Peter Ustinov   104
Barbara Cartland   104
Bob Guccione   107
Kenneth Tynan   107
Françoise Sagan   113

Sporting Life   115
Jimmy Connors   117
George Foreman   118
James Hunt   118
George Segal   121
George Best   121
David Niven   124

Couples   125
Rod Steiger   127
Jane Birkin and Serge
  Gainsbourg   127
Elke Sommer   132
Viscount and Lady
  Weymouth   132
Ryan O'Neal   139
Vidal and Beverly
  Sassoon   139

Stars of Stage and Screen	145	Gene Wilder	163
Pat Pheonix	147	Zsa Zsa Gabor	164
Richard Burton	151	Roger Moore	168
Oliver Reed	151	Dudley Moore	168
David Janssen	153	Elliott Gould	169
Marty Feldman	153	Gayle Hunnicutt	170
Robert Mitchum	155		
David Hemmings	155	*Postscript*	173
George Peppard	160	Dr. James Hemming	175
Glenda Jackson	160		

Acknowledgments

I am especially grateful to Desmond Wilcox for orginally encouraging me to go to America and write the G.I.B. book when it was just a few lines on paper and I was still a researcher at B.B.C. Television: and for his encouragement during the writing of this book.

I should like to thank Sybil Leek in Florida, Domenica Fitzgerald in Los Angeles, Margot George Comley in San Francisco, Eric Drache in Las Vegas and Ann Drache in New Jersey, for their invaluable hospitality and warmth. Debra Michael, Jenny Hearn and Rebecca Michael in London, for their industrious secretarial help. And the Inlingua Language School, Lake Constance for their translations of the French interviews.

I received introductions and help in arranging interviews from many people — they are too numerous to mention here, but I should like to thank them all — with special thanks to Vidal and Beverly Sassoon, and Sherry Grant in Los Angeles, Sue Hyman, Theo Cowan in London, and Yanou Collart in Paris. And for Martin Robertson whom I value both for his personal friendship and professional advice.

Introduction

I grew up during the 'sexual revolution'. In 1955 a single girl was 'cheap' if she went to bed with a man. In 1965 she was 'frigid' if she didn't. And in 1975 almost every woman did. Whereupon men discarded the question; 'Does she or doesn't she?' (go to bed) and replaced it with; 'Is she or isn't she?' (good in bed). Sexual attitudes had altered radically — and my own childhood and teens reflect the resultant changes and confusion.

I was six in 1956. 'The King and I' was the film of the year — 'Rock Around the Clock' was the record of the year — my father had an affair with a married beautician from Max Factor — and my mother told me about sex. I was left with the impression that sex existed exclusively for men and women who were married — preferably to each other. But that sex for the single girl was completely unthinkable.

Boarding school later consolidated that initial impression. The acid-faced English teacher, Mrs. Rogers, advised the Upper Fifth not to go to bed 'with the first man who pops his head around the corner — wait for him to pop a ring on your finger first.' And the Vicar held forth on 'petting' warning us; 'not below the neck, girls.' We just giggled — because sex was continually giggled about, whispered about and joked about. Science classes blossomed when a girl called Susan passed round newspaper reports of the Profumo Affair. Then we hid behind our desk lids and read about Christine Keeler and Mandy Rice Davies, single girls who not only had sex, but were even paid for it. We speculated briefly, but none of it seemed real, so we went back to 'Ready, Steady, Go' and Elvis Presley romancing Joan Blackman in 'Blue Hawaii.'

1965 — and the outside world had Twiggy, Mary Quant and Fanny Hill. Television unveiled the word 'fuck' — although at boarding school when a girl called Penny actually DID she was expelled instantly. Nevertheless, The Beatles continued to beg the school girls of the world to 'Please, Please Me' and 'Love Me Do' — while skirts got shorter and 'X' films sexier. London was described as 'swinging' and current society labelled as 'permissive'. Virginity was suddenly unfashionable — and sexual freedom was universally prescribed.

Although boarding school and 'O' Levels prevented me from experiencing life in the new 'permissive society', one of it's immediate consequences was characterised for me by Kenneth Tynan, during an interview for this book: 'At the height of the

3

swinging London scene, a girl told me that sexual liberty had been bad for her. She said; "I've been to bed with about 150 guys in the last 3 years and I've only had about 4 orgasms. Because nowadays if a guy says; "Let's go to bed" and you refuse – he'll say: "Fine" and just pass on to some other chick and make it with her within ten minutes. So you have to say yes – otherwise you miss out." '

1969 – and I finally emerged into a world where 'yes' appeared to be the only sexual language spoken. I went to university, where I encountered 'The Female Eunuch' the free 'Pill', 'Married Men Make the Best Lovers' and the one-night-stand. For many, sex preceeded relationships; first they took their daily 'Pill' – and then said 'yes' prematurely. Possibly at a party, where there were drinks, brief introductions, a dance or two, followed by bed. Then, maybe, a phone call the next day from the man. Sometimes he never phoned at all. Five years before, the man's silence could have been attributed to a flaw in the relationship – perhaps to a disagreement over dinner. Except that in 1969 there often wasn't any dinner – just bed. So day after day, many 'swinging sixties' girls waited for the phone to ring – and, when it didn't, felt sexually substandard, rejected and wondered where they had failed in their 'performance'; realising that in the new 'permissive society' relationships with men could be made or broken in bed.

Women had long ceased to worry about whether to 'go all the way' – the new concern was what to do once we got 'there'. My mother's generation had worried about pregnancy, my generation now worried about 'performance'. Women were still competing for male approval, except that the arena had switched from the kitchen to the bedroom. However, whereas every women used to have a recipe for the perfect pie, few of us possessed a recipe for perfect sex. And as sex was everywhere, along with rejections, vulnerability and insecurity, we all began searching for the perfect sexual ingredients. Naturally, the media was eager to supply them; suddenly there was 'The Sensuous Woman' the 'Sex Manners' series, – a barrage of 'How-to' books, a tremendous output of sexual information. The simplicity had gone out of sex – replaced by sexperts, sex techniques, and sex books.

1970 – and I lost my virginity three weeks before my 20th birthday, after which the man said I was 'very good'. His judgement flattered me, so I asked for a breakdown of my 'score'.

The man couldn't provide one, but just repeated that I was 'very good'. Thinking about it later, I realised that his pronouncement typified current sexual values; single women were now not only *expected* to go to bed, to know exactly what to do once they were *in* bed — but also to do it *well*. To be 'good in bed'.

My discovery that in the sexy yes-years of the seventies, men were actually grading women sexually, made me feel uneasy. Admittedly my present grade was apparently high — but supposing I was ever *downgraded* by a future man I cared about? Perhaps classified as 'bad in bed' and thereupon rejected. The consequences seemed monumental and I decided that I *had* to be 'good' for all time. I wished, though, that I knew the criteria governing male sexual ratings systems. I speculated, Was it face? figure? words? speed and ability to attain orgasm? staying power? skill at oral sex? secret sexual techniques?

Later — I talked to women of my own age and found them none the wiser. I discovered that although many were sexually experienced, they too felt the compulsion to be 'good in bed' — to be 'sexually perfect'. And the subsequent result was often sexual dissatisfaction. There were specific examples: Anna, who was repelled by group sex, yet allowed her husband to persuade her to take part, because she was afraid her refusal might lead him to a younger girl, who might agree, and therefore be thought by him to be 'better in bed.'

There was Lydia, submitting to anal sex, which she hated. Her boyfriend, whom she loved, had told her about a previous girlfriend who enjoyed anal sex and who had, as a result, been labelled 'good in bed'. So Lydia had anal sex for fear of being rejected. There was Mary, who went out with the same man for three years, but was still unable to tell him about her rape fantasies, afraid that he would think her odd and rate her 'bad in bed'. There was Susie, who nightly for two years, faked orgasms with her fiance. Unable to explain that she needed manual clitoral stimulation, because, as she confessed to me, she believed that sexy, 'good in bed' women orgasmed instantly through intercourse.

I was initially surprised to find such a high degree of sexual insecurity among the women I talked to. However, my small sample was validated two years later when 'The Hite Report' was published in America and I saw that my sample was a profile for any one of the 3,000 women who had completed Hite's

5

questionnaire on female sexuality. My interviews could in fact have been derived *from* 'The Hite Report' — which revealed identical female sexual insecurities.

After finishing my own interviews, I recognised that although female sexuality had theoretically been liberated and women's right to sexual pleasure conceeded, full sexual freedom and the route to sexual pleasure was still inhibited in many women, because they tried to conform to a 'good in bed' stereotype.

I decided to explore the subject further by asking men to define what *makes* a woman good in bed. I believed that the answers would provide commentaries on female sexual insecurities, proving them to be either justified or invalid. Although I hoped the replies would explode the 'good in bed' stereotype, I feared that they would perhaps contain certain common denominators, revealing a formula. None emerged, because the definitions of 'good in bed' were contrasting, diverse and very particular to each individual. Ultimately the attitudes were reassuring because the majority displayed a notable gap between what I and other women imagined men wanted sexually — and what men in reality wanted.

Eventually, I asked the man with whom I was then involved, and he outlined what makes a woman good in bed. Consequently, sex was discussed, desires and attitudes revealed, so helping the relationship become happier and more secure. I advised all my friends to ask the men with whom they were involved the same question. Many did, and the results were invariably reassuring, often revealing, and always instigated communication of mutual sexual desires. I began to feel that perhaps sexual freedom could be achieved for many women, and their insecurities and fears about not being 'good in bed' partially dispelled, by a discussion of what *makes* a woman 'good in bed'. By personalising in a book a generalisation used by men when discussing women.

INTERVIEWEE SELECTION

The Sexperts:

The first interviewees in this section are medical experts, chosen because of their work in the field of female sexuality. The gynecologist and the feminist were selected in order to discuss female attitudes to our own bodies and sexuality. The psychiatrist and the sex therapist were chosen because I believed that the advanced techniques with which they treat sexual problems might be informative.

The second series of interviewees in this section were chosen partly out of curiosity; prostitution may appear to be an anachronism in the so-called permissive society — yet seems to be on the increase. I wanted to discover what brand of 'good' men paid for. Also as many women I had talked to were intrigued by the mysteries of commercial sex, I wanted to explore the reality. First I interviewed two women operating in differing areas of prostitution: a call girl and ex-madam, Xaviera Hollander. Then I talked to two men representing ancient and modern forms of prostitution: the pimp, who in the past has controlled a large section of the trade, and the male prostitute (for women) who in the future may find his trade flourishing, as a result of female sexual liberation.

The Swinging Sixties, The Music World, Media Men and Women, Sporting Life, Couples, Stars of Stage and Screen.

These sections in my 'Gallup Poll with a difference' are composed of interviews with major celebrities. When I started the book, America and England were flooded with sex books and magazines. Large numbers of those sex magazines printed spicey letters from, 'R. S., Michigan', 'J. W., Oxford', and 'F. R., Houston'. The letters were extremely graphic, but the writer remained totally anonymous. Rumour was rife that many of these letters were concocted by sales conscious publishers. The whole effect was one of anonymity, unreality, saturation, and boredom.

I therefore decided to interview real identifiable people on their sexual attitudes, men and women with high visibility and curiosity value. As a journalist, I had already interviewed many leading celebrities, and had found that their general attitudes didn't differ radically from those of most people. However, their CHOICES were more numerous. The male celebrities were chosen not only because they symbolised the unattainable man, but also because their charisma and fame attract most women, giving them the potential for almost unlimited sexual experiences, and to meet the supposedly 'sexually perfect' woman. Men who women fantasise about. Men whose wives and lovers include some of the world's most desirable women. I chose men I personally was curious about, in terms of their life styles, images and sex appeal. And I expected that the desirability of these men would make them excessively critical and exacting when defining what makes a woman 'good in bed'.

The female celebrity interviewees were selected because of their resemblance to the stereotype, to the ideal 'good in bed' woman. Women whose glamour and beauty attract most men. Women whose lovers and husbands include some of the world's most desirable men. Women whom I believed might, through their beauty, fame and opportunity, hold the key to being 'good in bed'. Women I admired, and was curious about. Women whom men fantasise about.

TECHNIQUE

The interviews took place over a two year period in London, Los Angeles, Las Vegas, New York and Paris. During that time I interviewed over a hundred men and women, mostly in their own homes. The interviews, which were all taped, lasted from one hour to six. Each interview was later transcribed and then written in the form of a dramatised monologue.

In Hollywood I approached the celebrities personally and not through public relations agencies. My tactics were dictated by my experiences when I first arrived in California — I had first intended to write feature articles there, for British newspapers and magazines, and believed that my credentials and commisions were impressive. However, I discovered quickly that none of the P.R. people would arrange interviews, unless I represented 'Time Magazine' or 'People' — which I didn't. Even interviews for B.B.C. radio were impossible to set-up. After weeks of false promises and sincere propositions — 'I'll let you interview our clients if you go to bed with me, but unless you do, I won't' — I found myself intervieweeless, drowning in a sea of phone bills and letters from British magazines demanding to know why they hadn't received my Robert Redford interview.

Other journalists — either magazine staffers or freelances with financial backing — related experiences corresponding to my own. I felt very naive, having arrived in Hollywood with just $400, no driving licence and finally, no-where to live. There were, however, various solutions available. An ageing Persian millionaire offered me my own Hollywood apartment, in exchange for monthly 'scenes' with his Mexican girlfriend (who wore white lipstick and drank strawberry flavoured champagne). Then there was a greying married tycoon from the Trousdale Estate who promised me $200 a week, provided that I meet him every Thursday at his rented suite at the Beverly Wilshire Hotel (where he could deal with urgent business calls if necessary). And a Las Vegas taxi driver offered me $500 'a time' ('on behalf of a major hotel') to cater to the whims of visiting V.I.P. gamblers, and presented me with his card. All three offers were rejected.

Fortunately, I had the opportunity to research a sober B.B.C. documentary on Charles Manson which terrified me, was never produced, but still paid for meals. Then I investigated pregnancy testing clinics for the 'National Enquirer', interviewed Mae West for the B.B.C., and spent half a day on the telephone trying to sell 'Bicentennial biros' to undertakers.

Nevertheless, my money still ran out — and I discovered that American banks don't give overdrafts, American phone companies disconnect telephones, and American landlords evict tenants. Finally, I ended up sleeping on the floor of a Malibu nudist camp, in the middle of December. Then I house-sat for two lesbians (at that time, meditating in Big Sur), fed their two gold fish ('light and dark'), and talked to the Buddhist upstairs (reputedly a relative of the Hearsts) who had long hair and a bun. Robert Redford seemed a million miles away. Eventually though, things brightened, when a friend (a well-known witch and psychic) invited me to her home in Florida, because she had received strong premonitions about my book project.

Encouraged, I returned to Hollywood, borrowed the minimum money for survival, and finally began to write the book; conscious that if B.B.C. radio interviews had been difficult to arrange, then interviews for a 'sex book' would be impossible. Predictably, none of the American interviews were arranged by a P.R. person. Some were set-up after endless phone calls to the celebrity's home, others after 'Celebrity Bulletin' had published details of a celebrity's arrival, the name of their hotel, so that I could telephone them. Others were arranged by personal introduction. Sometimes I even approached the celebrities 'cold' at various Hollywood parties and functions, where I introduced myself, described the subject of my book, asked for an interview, then held my breath and looked hopeful. Surprisingly, perhaps, even people who wouldn't agree to be interviewed still gave me their definitions. I felt that perhaps many celebrities agreed to talk to me because they were bored with discussing their latest film – Elliott Gould even said 'its great to talk about the subject'.

Las Vegas was easier. Virtually P.R. free, the performers relax and mingle quite freely with the guests at the large hotels. Perhaps I should have gambled in Las Vegas – because luck seemed to be with me; I was taken to see Engelbert Humperdinck in one of the showrooms, sat in the front row, and at the end of the performance, he chose a girl to come up on stage with him. Out of 1100 people, Engelbert unaccountably chose me, sung to me, then invited me backstage – giving me the ideal opportunity to ask for a definition of what makes a woman 'good in bed'.

After the horrors and humiliations of Hollywood, my European interviews were simpler to arrange. The American version of the book hadn't yet been published, but I still received help from press agents in London and Paris, and was relieved to no longer be Miss-No-One-from-No-Where with just an implausible book idea and no publisher.

Once the interviews were arranged, they all went extremely smoothly. I played the moment and the person, as opposed to their publicity and press cuttings, and none of my interviewees ever refused to answer a question. I never started an interview with the all-embracing question, 'What makes a woman good in bed?' Instead, my 'ice-breaker' question for men was, 'Can you tell if a woman is good before you touch her?' and for women the question was usually, 'When did you first hear the phrase "good in bed"?'

The questions were never written down and were always varied. However, in general, my questions to male interviewees were aimed at eliciting comments and opinions on those aspects of sexuality about which women felt insecure. Questions to female interviewees were generally aimed at producing a reflection of that particular woman's sexual self-image.

Specific questions I asked the male celebrities often included the following: 'Describe the woman who is "bad" in bed.' 'Does the woman who is "good" ever refuse anything in bed?' 'Is a woman less "good" if she asks for what she wants?' 'Can a woman learn to be "good"?' 'Can a woman be non-orgasmic and yet still be "good"?' 'Is a woman less "good" if she takes a long time to come?' 'Is the woman who is "good", "good" the first time she goes to bed with a man?' 'Is there any particular age group of woman most likely to be "good in bed"?' 'Is there a physical type of woman most likely to be "good in bed"?' 'What is the relationship between beauty and "good in bed"?' 'If you were Dr. Frankenstein and able to create the "ideal" woman in bed, what would she be like?' 'How rare is the "good in bed" woman?'

I asked the female celebrities questions that included: 'Have you ever worried about being "good"?' 'Have men ever made you feel sexually inadequate?' 'Have you ever been afraid to ask for what you want in bed?' 'Have you ever been afraid to refuse what you don't want?' 'Do you feel less "good" if you take a long time to come?' 'Have you ever faked in bed?' 'Have you changed sexually with age?' 'Do you think there is a difference between what a man terms "good in bed" and what is "good" in your own view?' 'What advice would you give to other women who want to be "good"?'

My questions to the medical experts were aimed at eliciting reaction to female sexual insecurities, relating in particular to our own bodies, as well as advice, and, hopefully, reassurance. My questions to the prostitutes centred mostly on technique hints, and on the relationship between prostitute and client.

RESULTANT THEMES AND ATTITUDES

The Sexperts:

The major theme stressed by the medical sexperts is the importance of communication in attaining sexual happiness and compatability. The 'prostitute' sexperts supply explicit sexual techniques — but also, surprisingly, reassurance; one of the book's strongest themes (reflected also in 'The Hite Report') is the female fear of refusing a disliked sexual practice. For example many women (including a leading sex therapist) told me they disliked swallowing male ejaculate after oral sex. They still did so, in order not to reject the man and consequently be 'bad' in bed. Yet I interviewed high priced prostitutes who told me that not only did they refuse to swallow but that even in commercial transactions, the customer never demanded his money back.

The Celebrity Interviews:

As its title suggests, the book's most prevalent note is one of frankness: Angie Bowie describes how she and David were late for their own wedding, because they were having sex with a girl, Michael Parkinson describes how he lost his virginity and Roger Daltry details his sexual experiences with four groupies at once. There are countless other examples which contribute to the book on an often sensational level. Sexual insecurities are admitted by such differing female celebrities as Bianca Jagger, Jilly Cooper, Jane Birkin and Pat Pheonix; women whose images led me to expect the reverse. And for me personally, one of the book's major surprises lies in the often startling contrast between a celebrity's image, and the reality revealed by their interview.

Specific Themes and Attitudes:

The end-product is a kaleidescope of contrasting sexual themes, attitudes, prejudices and beliefs relating to, among others: the Permissive Society, Woman's Liberation, pornography, prositut-tion, lesbian relationships, masturbation, vibrators, oral sex, anal sex, orgies and sex fantasies. The sexual education of children, sex and athletes, sex and the beautiful woman, sex and the successful man and woman, sex and the experienced woman, sex and the vir-gin, sex and the older men and women. The relationship between sex and love, between sex and romance. Sex without love, sexual expectations versus reality, sexual failure, sex and mystery. Male and female attitudes to one-night stands, female refusals to have sex. 'Good in bed' related to experience, to age, to beauty. Male and female reactions to the first time they go to bed with a new partner. Advice on how to be 'good in bed'. Male and female attitudes to the orgasm, to faking orgasms, to the multi-orgasm, to the time it takes to orgasm, to orgasmic impairment.

Attitudes regarding sexual communication, and requesting or refusing sexual practices. One of the book's most emphasised attitudes relates to the pros and cons of a woman asking for what she wants in bed. Therefore, I have used it here as a way of illustrating how the book may be read, following just one specific theme in order to gain a perspective on attitudes to the problem.

James Hunt: 'If a woman wants something particular and doesn't ask for it — what am I supposed to do? Am I supposed to read her mind and guess? So I always like a woman to ask for what she wants, and do it.

Jane Birkin: 'A lot of women have got imagination but are a bit scared to ask for the things they have imagined. I was lucky to find somebody who had imagination and the same ideas as I had and didn't think I was stupid. Otherwise I don't think I would have had the courage to jump on someone and say, "I've always wanted to see what it would be like to have it off in the bathroom".'

Elliott Gould: 'It's great if a woman asks for what she wants in bed. I love a woman who is point blank — specific!'

Mandy Rice Davis: 'I don't agree with talking a lot in bed and I don't use words to turn a man on, although its important for a woman to be able to ask for what she wants in bed. She should always wait for the right opportunity though. For example, it is easier to make sexual demands on those evenings when two people are very turned on and are at an ideal point in their relationship. But when a woman meets a man for the first time, she should never make demands.'

Patrick Lichfield: 'A woman is enormously helpful if she asks for what she wants in bed. Its lovely, its absolutely marvellous. You don't pick up a camera without reading the instruction manual first. You want to see what it can do. Provided that she doesn't like something that is either impossibly uncomfortable or continually wants to do something that is vaguely against your nature, or what you would generally call "unnatural", and provided it isn't something you actually don't like doing. But if you know what turns the woman on its a winner.'

Justin de Villeneuve: 'I feel insecure if a girl asks for what she wants in bed.'

David Hemmings: 'There is no question that a woman should ask for what she wants in bed. But she has to time her demands according to the mood and conditions. You have to openly discuss what you both require and desire.'

Oliver Reed: 'I think a woman is possibly less good if she asks for what she wants in bed. A woman always wants to be dominated in bed, but is afraid to admit it.'

Zsa Zsa Gabor: 'When you are in bed with a man you love or are attracted to, you don't have to talk about what you like — everything comes naturally. The best way to lose a man is not to let him be his natural self.'

There are contrasting opinions even in the same home.

Vidal Sassoon: 'I think hot blooded women who make demands can be very exciting.'

Beverly Sassoon: 'I don't think you need to *ask* for what you want in bed. I think if a woman has got any sort of intelligence, she can lead a man into doing what she wants.'

Viscount Weymouth: 'An inclination towards experimentation makes a woman good, but I personally prefer it if the initiation comes from myself. I wouldn't downgrade a woman who asked for what she wanted in bed, but I like a woman who enables me to play through my culturally imposed role. I have been brought up in the culture of the male setting the pace — rightly or wrongly. So that if I feel that I am not initiating the relationship, that the woman is setting the pace, I feel emasculated and I might not even get an erection.'

Pat Pheonix: 'I think when sex gets to the time of having to say words like, "You strike position 2 and I'll strike position 1" then it's no longer romantic.'

14

Kenneth Tynan: 'There are a great many things one can do in cars on a motorway — *you* would be astonished and *I* would probably be arrested. And the woman who is good suggests her own scenes, you infect each other with ideas.'

Michael Parkinson: 'If a woman wants something else specific in bed, then you will find out by trial and error, and that discovery is one of the deepest mysteries of sex.'

Imogen Hassall: 'Of course asking for what you want in bed is very difficult if you play the servant role — so I would wait until I found the man who gave me what I wanted. Usually though I would be very amicable — I would ask the man to tell me what he wanted — then I would say what I wanted. Asking for head is very difficult though — I don't think many men want to do it — they don't mind you doing it to them though, for ages.'

Bianca Jagger: 'You shouldn't have to ask for what you want in bed. I hate words. I think that if you have any amount of communication and understanding you don't have to use words unless the man is selfish and assumes things are due to him and not the woman.'

Isaac Hayes: 'Sometimes a woman will not do something because she is afraid of what the man will think of her. So I think that the man should really tell the woman up-front, "Hey, whatever you want to do, you tell me, you tell me what you want to do, whatever you do is alright". Women should ask for what they want and not expect a man to be a know-it-all.'

Jilly Cooper: 'Women often lack the guts to ask for what they want in bed because they are subservient. The good person in bed creates an emotional atmosphere in which their partner is relaxed enough to ask for what they want or admit being unhappy or worried. I think everybody is inclined to gloss sex over and not have the guts to say; "I'd like you to dress up as a Vicar." People should discuss what they want early on in a relationship — because if you don't and if you suddenly after five years say, "That is repulsive to me" or "Why didn't you do such and such?" It's terrible.'

15

REACTIONS TO THE BOOK

A version of this book was published in America under the title; 'What makes a woman G.I.B. (good in bed)' and critics labelled it 'A celebrity Kinsey Report'. On publication I did a nationwide radio and T.V. tour of America. During the many discussion and phone-in programmes, I discovered that women, as I had originally hoped, were using the book as a channel for sexual communication; celebrity sexual frankness providing a springboard to general discussions of sex. The book enabled many women to lead the conversation from celebrity sexual attitudes and problems, to their own. Both men and women told me that they used the book as a means of discovering their partner's sexual desires; simply by asking which celebrity attitude their partner most agreed with and, at the same time, volunteering their own favoured celebrity attitude, so that they were able to communicate their own sexual desires.

Hopefully 'Speaking Frankly' will produce a similar reaction in Britain. But also I would like to think that it will be read as a reflection of the contemporary sexscape, changing sexual attitudes and roles, thus providing a commentary on current trends within sex and relationships, and that it will also clarify some of the sexual confusion in which my generation and I grew up.

The Sexperts

SEX THERAPIST

Although men and women with serious sexual problems often consult sex therapists in America, very few male therapists are currently recognised as legitimate. Therefore women often visit female sex therapists for advice. I talked to a leading New York sex therapist, British-born Pauline Abrams. Before the interview, Pauline — a very bubbly lady from North London — treated a male client called Jeffrey, and after it, discussed orgasmic impairment with her next client, a 28 year old girl, Suzanne.

I am 38. When I was growing up, a woman didn't have to be good in bed — she just had to be *married*. We were told that once we were married, we could go to bed; then, when we were finally *in* bed we were allowed to open our legs. But no one ever told us that we were expected to open them *well*. Today's generation are growing up with the idea that they have to be good. This creates tremendous pressures and performance anxieties every time they go to bed, ultimately making them just as tense as the older generation.

Women believe all sorts of garbage about what makes them good in bed; that they have to give a man an erection at the drop of a hat, that they themselves have to be instantly orgasmic. Women have been raised to feel that sex is not their due, so they will let men do anything that isn't painful, even though they may be uncomfortable or bored. Women also tend to think; 'If I were really good in bed, he would never want to sleep with another woman.' — and that being good means being the best.

The woman who really *is* good in bed is often recognisable because she is prepared to talk freely to her partner about her own personal sexual experiences. There are so many conflicting opinions, and I don't believe a man can tell if a woman is good in bed unless he talks to her.

There is no correlation between the size of a woman's clitoris and her sexual enjoyment or orgasmic capacity. In fact, there are very few absolutes governing the woman who is good in bed. I think she has to enjoy sex, because if she doesn't, her partner won't. She has to enjoy oral sex, and she has to be sensual, responsive, and abandoned, with the capacity for communication.

The woman who is good is abandoned. She is vocal, makes

noises, and does not feel ashamed of any part of her body, or any-thing that is part of the sex act. She has to abandon herself to lust, and not many people can do that. Being good is not a tech-nique – it is a way of responding, of feeling good about your partner and being sensitive to his needs. The woman who is good is responsive in bed, but being responsive does *not* necessarily mean being orgasmic. The orgasm is not a response to the man's excellent technique; it is the result of a multiplicity of factors.

Being orgasmic is not what makes a woman good in bed. There are some men who believe it does; but men like that don't really give a damn about the woman – it's their own ego that is invested in the woman's orgasms – and those men wear the woman's orgasms like medals on their chests. They place pressure on a woman to come, as in the old Lenny Bruce line: 'Did you come? Did you come? Did you come, come, come?'; in fact the woman's orgasmic capacity is totally irrelevant to the question of whether or not she is good in bed.

Some women are just not very orgasmic, but some women feel less good if they fail to have an orgasm. Other women have a credit system where they feel the man owes them an orgasm; unless these women come, they feel that they didn't get their money's worth. That's absurd, because few men are responsible for the physiological capacity their partner has for orgasm.

I feel that a woman is responsible for her own orgasm. If she doesn't come, and it bothers her, she should masturbate. That will make some men insecure, but those men are insecure to begin with. I like to give my vibrator to my lover. But I have my best orgasms if I put a dildo inside me, so that it touches my cervix, and then use the vibrator. That makes my orgasms much stronger.

There is no fixed timespan for each individual's orgasm. It always varies, but women are constantly bugged by thinking, 'Is he bored?' 'How do I know he is enjoying what he is doing?' 'Maybe he really wants to stop?' I am just like any other woman and I feel the same way until I have built up a strong relationship of trust. Sometimes I don't come at all. When a woman worries ('Maybe his hand is tired?' 'Maybe his mouth is tired?'), she stops her orgasm or slows it down.

The orgasmic timespan is different with every woman at dif-ferent times. It even alters in masturbation. Some days I come in thirty seconds; other days I know exactly what it's like to be an impotent male; I put my hand on my clitoris and I can't feel a thing. It takes longer for me to come with a vibrator, because I can't control the feedback system as well as with my own hand. The feedback system is also far less reliable when some other hand is on you; you get very, very close and if you were masturbating yourself you would know exactly what to do. You may have been close to an orgasm a hundred times, but the man keeps going off a fraction. It's annoying.

Women take no longer to achieve orgasm during masturbation than men; but in intercourse the feedback system is much less accurate for women than it is for men because the slightest error in movement takes the hand away from the centre of excitation, which is the clitoris.

Every woman has a different kind of orgasm. Some women are multiorgasmic, and each orgasm becomes more and more powerful. So they keep wanting orgasms, because the next one is always better than the last. Women like that often have orgasms that appear very meaningless, and sometimes they don't even know that they have come.

I have an orgasm like a man: once I have had it, my libido is spent and I am not interested in sex for quite a while. So I would much rather continue to make love and not have my orgasm. I once had a marvellous lover who suddenly announced that he was going to make me multiorgasmic. But, knowing that my orgasm was so vital for him (this wasn't conscious), I never came at all with him.

There are partners with whom I am 100 percent orgasmic — nothing gets in the way; my head never works, just my body. Trust matters, but it can work negatively. Some women have affectional response. They can't come with men they love and they are unable to abandon themselves because they feel that the man is judging them, whereas they can abandon themselves totally and come very easily with men they don't give a damn about.

I am not always orgasmic, especially if the trust has been destroyed. My second husband was very virile. I used to come as soon as he did, and he would still have an erection afterwards. Then we were divorced, but we still continued an affair. One day, in a moment of anger, he said: 'Sex therapist, sex therapist, for *years* I have been faking.' And then he told me that he had faked

21

orgasm in order to get me to come. I don't know how true that was, but once he had told me, I never came with my ex-husband again, ever. Every time he came I would think, 'Maybe he is faking,' and so I became nonorgasmic with the same man with whom I had always been 100 percent orgasmic.

I've still got places to go sexually – I become increasingly more abandoned each year. Sexual growth is in a state of flux, it's very dynamic and we never stop growing. Experimentation leads to sexual growth, and the woman who is good will always experiment. She will be open to fantasies, role playing, and dressing up (men really do like women in black garters and silk stocking). The woman who is good should accommodate her partner's sex fantasies and live out her own; she should try everything a few times (I don't know what a few times is, but I sure as hell know it means more than once or twice).

Men want to try anal sex; the woman who is good will give it a try until she can objectively make up her mind. I don't like swallowing male ejaculate, but if I am in a relationship for a lengthy period of time and it appears important to the man for me to swallow, I try. I have discovered that telling a man that swallowing his ejaculate makes me throw up generally makes him incapable of ejaculating in my mouth in the future. Men are as sensitive as women, and caring lovers do not want to put their partners through any unpleasant experiences. Usually though, unless they have to come in the open air, men don't mind if I fail to swallow their ejaculate – it just has symbolic connotations. After a lengthy period of oral sex, most men are quite content to come in the woman's vagina.

A lesbian experience can teach a woman that her cunt is sensuous, not slimy and smelly. When a woman inserts her tongue or finger into another woman's cunt, she will find that it is really warm and moist and womblike. Her attitude alters. Ninety percent of all women hate their own genitals, and are ashamed of them. That's very common to women – I see surrogates who think that their cunts are ugly. But no man ever thinks his penis is ugly – he thinks it is the most important gift to women, that it rules the world. Women have a much more negative body image than men, especially in this glamour culture. I work in the nude most of the time, and I am very comfortable with my own body, but most women are not.

It is impossible to be good in bed if you have a bad body image. I teach a three-day workshop, and one of the courses is in sex conscousness-raising. People are surprisingly ashamed of their bodily functions: farting, having to go to the bathroom, using almost the same equipment with which they go to the bathroom for sex. They feel guilty and ashamed.

Through therapy and education I teach people to stop letting their heads bother them, to be freer. I teach techniques in communication. The woman who is good is able to communicate her sexual desires. I teach people to say the things that embarrass them. For example: 'I would love to go down on you, but would you mind taking a shower first?' Or, 'I'd love to kiss you, but would you mind brushing your teeth first?' People have incredible problems regarding sexual communication.

Women are also very ignorant about their own bodies. They are unfamiliar with their functions. For example, every woman who wants to be good should insert her finger in her vagina and taste her own vaginal mucuosa for cleanliness. I don't think she should go to bed before she has tasted herself, just as she shouldn't go to bed before she has brushed her teeth. A woman should also become familiar with the man's sexual functions; she should remember that men differ sexually according to their age.

Boys of eighteen are tremendously anxious. They get erections easily, but they can lose them through nervousness. The older man maintains his erection, but he may not always ejaculate every time he has intercourse. The amount of ejaculate is lessened, as is its strength. Most importantly, the older man doesn't respond very cerebrally, and he requires more tactile stimulation. He doesn't get turned on by looking at a naked woman – he gets turned on when she touches him. It is unrealistic for a woman to lie down next to an older man and expect him to respond instantly with an erection.

The woman who is bad in bed has high, unrealistic expectations of a man. She is a castrating bitch and criticises him constantly. We have patients whose girlfriends always sit in judgement over them. Then the men becomes terrified of every move he makes. The woman deballs him; she is bad because she is ignorant.

Embarrassment at her own body and her sexual feelings make a woman bad. She doesn't move, she hates her own body, and she doesn't make sounds. She doesn't communicate verbally, and she fails to respond. She has bad muscle tone in her vagina, and she is unable to grip the man with it. The woman who is good, however, thinks of her vagina as a sensuous tool which she uses to give a man pleasure; therefore she exercises to improve its muscle tone.

The ultimate virtue of the woman who is good in bed is that she has no fixed criteria for being good. The woman who is good doesn't take a set of rules to bed with her. She knows that every sexual experience is unique and that every time she goes to bed, even with the same person, the sex will be different. There are only two kinds of sex − good and bad − and good sex is always different.

FEMINIST: SELF-EXAMINATION GROUPS

Over the past four years, Carol Downer of the Los Angeles Feminist Health Centre has taught hundreds of women the techniques of vaginal self-examination with the use of a mirror and a speculum. The aim is to help women familiarise themselves with their own bodies and gynecological functions. The examinations are held in groups at the centre, and the women who attend are mostly radical feminists.

The stereotype of a woman who is good in bed is still a woman who reflects a man's desires. I believe that every woman has done something at one time in her life in order to be good in bed: letting a man touch her when she didn't want him to, having sex when she felt tired, not asking for what she wanted in bed. At the centre we have been measuring our libidos, and some of us find that we rarely have sex at the times when our libidos are at their height, because the timing of sex is determined by the man's libido − when *he* wants to have sex.

Sometimes, just for fun, I will ask a self-examination group to raise their hands if they have *never* faked an orgasm. I have never yet seen a hand raised by any woman.

A lot of women fake because they are afraid to say that they didn't come, so they just give up and fake. Women fake all the time in bed, to be good for men. I don't think most women get orgasms with straight fucking anyway, mostly just manually or orally.

Women have to alter their attitudes to their genitals before they

24

can really enjoy sex, to forget those years of not looking at their sex organs and being taught to keep their skirts over their knees while their male peers were comparing each other's penises. The whole attitude of women to their genitals is one of self-disgust. Women know more about a man's penis, are more willing to touch it, than they are willing to touch or look at their own sex organs. Learning to like a penis and dislike their own sex organs is a cultivated taste that women develop over a period of time, just as people learn to appreciate classical music.

It is very dramatic when we do self-examination. The women go from mild shock and distaste to intense curiosity. At first, some women have difficulty even in opening their legs, they are so conditioned to keeping them closed. Women *do* worry about being good in bed, but what they really mean by that is 'pleasing the man.' But before they can even do that they need to recover from years of self-disgust. Our conditioning still takes over; one of the women in the group lost total control the first time a man gave her oral sex, and she urinated. The man accepted it, but the self-disgust remains for her, and for the many other women who are ashamed of their own bodies and their sexuality.

PSYCHOLOGIST: ASSERTIVENESS TRAINING GROUPS

Assertiveness training groups meet all over America. The training aims to teach men and women how to get what they want and refuse what they don't want — without feeling guilty. The training lasts over 12 hours and the group I observed contained a high proportion of women. I interviewed Dr. Stuart Fischoff, a doctor of psychology at Cal. State University and one of the founders of the group, Assertion Unlimited, on how the training can be applied to sex.

I have found women are more afraid of failure in bed than men are. They are afraid that they won't have orgasms, or that they won't be able to let a man know how much they are enjoying sex. I once knew a girl who couldn't get an orgasm at all quickly. She felt so badly about this, that it affected her whole way of relating to men. She developed a style, a way of satisfying a man,

25

because she was afraid he would reject her as soon as he realized that she was unable to have an orgasm quickly.

The area of sex is very sensitive. In order for a woman to have a better chance of achieving sexual satisfaction in bed, she has to be willing to take the risk of telling her partner what satisfies her. So she has to be assertive, open, honest and willing to take a risk. The best way for a woman to get what she wants in bed, or to avoid what she doesn't want, and still be 'good' for the man, is to approach all sexual problems verbally. Many people engage in a conspiracy of silence about their sexual needs. A man gets sexual satisfaction from knowing that a woman is enjoying sex and being satisfied, so her being open to him about her needs will further that end. It is also important for the woman to forget about the fantasy many women still have, which is that the man will be alienated by her requests or refusals. No one is that powerful and able to alienate and hurt another person very badly. However, the verbal techniques of coping with sex have to be learned — you don't, for example, approach your partner and say 'My last boyfriend used to . . .'

The best way to talk about sex is out of bed, and to find out what a man likes first. Picture a situation where, as is fairly common, the woman gives the man oral sex, but doesn't know how to ask for it without tarnishing the 'good in bed' image.

This is how I would suggest the woman approach the situation, via the use of assertive language:

The couple have just had sex and are lying in bed. . .

Woman: I really feel close to you.
Man: I am glad.
Woman: Do you ever talk to the women you are with about what you want in bed?
Man: No.
Woman: Do you think they know?
Man: They should.
Woman: Well, I would like to know what makes you happy.
Man: Everything you do.
Woman: I don't believe that. I think there are some things you like more than others. Because there are some things I like more than others. People I have been with have had special preferences as well.

Man: Well, I have never had any preference problems. I like it all.

Woman: Aren't there times when you have better orgasms than others?

Man: No — all orgasms are great.

Woman: That's funny, because I know for myself that I sometimes have better orgasms than others, and a lot of times it is due to where the man touches me. I know that it is the same with men, that sometimes I might touch their penises wrongly so that it hurts.

Man: What are you trying to tell me? Did I do something wrong?

At this point the woman must avoid making the man feel too defensive. It is advisable to proceed by trying to find out how to satisfy him, and once you have done that, he will naturally ask questions about what satisfies you:

Woman: I guess it is important for me to know what makes you happy in bed, and I would love you to tell me.

Once you start hitting the man with the positive, by telling him what you like about his sexual approach and by asking him what else he feels he would like you to do, he will feel reinforced, and will lower his defenses for oral sex.

You have to start right at the beginning of a relationship by asking for what you want, and finding out what he wants. The trap is waiting too long for good sex to develop, till the relationship gets into a sexual rut. There IS a risk in talking, but there is a guaranteed sexual mismatch if you don't.

Some women are afraid to ask for things in bed they imagine might be thought kinky, but there are ways of testing the other person's receptiveness:

Woman: I dreamed last night that I went to bed with two men at once. It really turned me on, but I have never tried it.

This gives the man a chance to know what the woman is interested in without feeling threatened, because the whole idea is couched in a dream.

The other major problem for women is fear of refusing a sexual practice they dislike, or are unprepared for, in case they alienate the man and are thought not to be good in bed. This is the way the situation can be handled with assertiveness training:

Man: Next time we get together, I have a friend I would like to join us, so that the three of us can get it together. I get turned on by the idea of two women, and I love the idea of two women doing things to me at once. So next time, I'll arrange for her to come over, because you will love it.

Woman: You want the three of us to go to bed together? I have thought about that . . .

Man: I am glad you have thought about it — you will love it.

Woman: I really feel uncomfortable about the whole thing.

Man: But this woman is so good and so are you, and so am I. After a few minutes you will really be into it. I am planning on it and I don't see what your problem is.

Woman: I guess the problem is that I don't really want to do it. I don't feel comfortable.

Man: Have you ever tried it?

Woman: No.

Man: So how do you know that you don't feel comfortable, if you have never tried it. You feel safe with me, so trust me.

Woman: I guess I don't feel able to trust you in this situation. I have to trust my feelings and at this point I don't want to get involved in a threesome.

Man: Are you saying that you never want to?

Woman: No. I am saying that right now I don't.

Man: But I am telling you it is something that I like. If you are going to be involved with me and we are going to be together, I really expect it. I want to please you — you ought to try and please me.

Woman: I think that pleasing each other is very important. I would never want to do anything that would displease you and I hope that you would never want to do anything to displease me.

Man: But you have never done it, so you don't know if it would displease you.

Woman: I also have never chopped someone's head off and I know that would displease me — I just don't want to.

Man: I really think you have a problem.

Woman: I might. I just don't see it that way. I don't want to get involved with more than one person in bed.

28

Man: That makes me very unhappy, because I was really planning on doing it. And I thought you were a groovy woman, really good in bed.

Woman: I guess that if wanting to have sex with two people is being good in bed, then I am not. But I really like sex with you.

The man is using every manipulative technique in the book to get what he wants and the woman is dealing with it well. The man's aim is to make the woman feel inadequate and insecure by making her have guilt but also flattering her. However, she has separated the guilt and the flattery from the demand she doesn't want to give in to. Most women would still give in, and be good at the cost of their own pleasure and self-respect, which really defeats the whole purpose of sex.

DR. MARTIN COLE

Dr. Martin Cole runs the Institute for Sex Education and Research, in Birmingham, a centre for the treatment and advice for men and women with sexual problems. Dr. Cole employs female surrogates, but also acts as a surrogate himself, in order to treat female patients who suffer from sexual dysfunctions. We met at his house in Birmingham, drank coffee in a relaxed atmosphere, with Dr. Cole talking freely about his own sexual preferences, in a conversation that veered between the personal and the medical.

Any girl is going to be good in bed if she makes me feel good — that's all. I would define a woman as being good in bed if she pleases me. It's not her that matters — it's if I feel safe, relaxed, reassured and unthreatened — that I can talk to the woman and don't want to run away afterwards.

Good in bed may be an experience in which the man is satisfied, but the woman may not have enjoyed the sex at all. But if you are preoccupied with pleasing your partner, you are in for a hell of a problem — because you are thinking. The most terrible thing a man or a woman can do is to think about their partner. If a man is thinking of the woman then he is going to turn himself off. And the greatest compliment anyone can pay to their partner is to be turned on. If a woman wants to be good in bed she should forget that objective because if she sets out in a thinking way to work a strategy it will be counter-productive. She must never think of her partner, only of herself and her own needs, then she will be able to give. Both men and women should behave in unselfconscious, autonomous giving and taking ways. Not thinking. Not timing and measuring their partner's response.

I personally prefer it if a woman doesn't have an orgasm. If she does, it's great, but if she doesn't, it's even greater, because then I am not under any obligation to give her one. Take, for example, three women: the first is orgasmic the minute you show her a penis — which is fine — except that the experience is likely to be over quickly, because that kind of woman tends to lose interest after her orgasm. Then there is the second woman who orgasms after half an hour. You go to bed with that woman a couple of times then you realise that she takes half an hour to orgasm, therefore the experience has a time factor built-in. So you thump away, you may enjoy it and you may not, but you still have a contract. But if a girl says, 'I never get orgasms' you don't have to worry at all. Also there is the challenge of 'She might have an orgasm with me'.

I act as a surrogate with a number of my female patients. There was one girl who had never been orgasmic during intercourse. I saw her several times, and eventually she had a fantastic orgasm. Months later, I met her and she said, 'By the way, I faked it.' So I had to amend my records . . . Really I think that the only way you can tell if a woman has orgasmed is by the amount of noise she makes. However, some women have very quiet orgasms which are still very satisfying for them.

One can regard the clitoris as a microphone — and the loud-speaker as being where you get the sensation during orgasm. This can either be the clitoris itself, or the vagina. Some women only get orgasms in their clitoris, other women get them in their entire pelvic area, which then goes into contractions. The type of orgasm a woman has is closely related to her body build and to her personality; very slim girls will usually have largely clitorial orgasms, whereas large girls will have vaginal and uterinal orgasms. There are also two types of personalities; the parasympathetic and the sympathetic. The parasympathetic personality likes sex and responds orgasmically in the vagina. She is fond of creature comforts, sleeps well, and tends to have a reasonable appetite.

The sympathetic personality tends to be slim, anxious, and a great worrier. When this type of women is orgasmic she tends to have localised clitoral orgasms.

These are generalisations but I think extroverts will be more sexual than introverts. So will those people who are both extrovert and neurotic, who seek experience in a kind of frenetic way. The whole way a woman responds sexually is intimately related to all her other personality characteristics. A woman is born good − not made, you don't acquire sexual skills − you develop them but the potential for sexuality is inborn, not a learnt response.

The older woman, if she has retained her attractiveness, is likely to be a good partner. She is likely to be more confident and able to achieve orgasm, having lost the arrogance of youth and being able to give.

A lot of beautiful women are not good in bed. The reason is that there is often an inverse relationship between attractiveness and sexual aggression. Women produce two hormones; oestrogens and androgens. Oestrogen makes a woman attractive, androgens make her active. The ideal is a high oestrogen/high androgen woman who will therefore be attractive AND sexually active. But often there is an inverse relationship because androgens and oestrogens are antagonistc and therefore cancel each other out. So that if you have a woman who has high oestrogen and low androgen, she will be very attractive, but she won't be sexually active. However, if a woman has got high androgens and low oestrogens, she won't be very attractive but very active sexually. Most people are well-balanced, but to generalise, if you have a woman who is somewhat masculine, with very prominent features, she will tend to be sexually active, unless she is so inhibited that she has sublimated her sex drive into a career. Sometimes women like that never have the opportunity to release their sexuality − are spinsters − but given the opportunity, would be instantly orgasmic.

We try and think of euphemisms for frigidity, but it does exist. There are women who have been brought up to feel they are not sexual − who don't 'spark' when they are touched, and who suffer from orgasmic dysfunction. We first teach that kind of woman to achieve orgasm by herself with a vibrator. We also ask her to fake, to act out her orgasm at the appropriate moment. By doing that she will distract herself, and is then more likely to orgasm.

31

If the woman has a regular partner we suggest that she masturbates in front of him. A lot of women do seem to block when the penis enters the vagina — out of fear of being filled up. So it is a matter of desensitising these women progressively. So after the woman learns to masturbate in front of her partner, she then learns to masturbate with the penis in the entrance of her vagina. Until eventually she orgasms with the penis actually inside the vagina.

If the woman is married, and comes to us for help, the problem is usually complete sexual boredom, that she is no longer getting aroused. She is sexually bored, and wants an escape route. The important thing is to emphasise to her that she hasn't got a problem. If the relationship between the woman and her partner is good it must be preserved, but there is no reason for the woman to do without sex. So we introduce that woman to another partner. We wrap it up and present the experience as treatment — which gives the woman permission. At least she will discover that in certain sexual situations she *can* operate. What she does with that information depends on her own values and it may take years for her to develop a compromise.

Treating sexual disorders in an individual is easier than treating two people within the context of their relationship. In the case of a couple, you have to deal with a man, a woman and a relationship — so that what might be good for one may not be good for the other. The single woman, as she gets older, will find that she has age on her side — with her chances of achieving orgasm increasing with time. And if she follows her intuitive need to experiment sooner or later she will find somebody who rewards not only her physical needs but also her psychic needs.

Women should tell a man their sexual fantasies, and get him to describe his. If a man or a woman wants to discover their partner's fantasies, they should describe a series of fantasies while screwing and then ask their partner to choose the one he likes best. So that verbal exploration leads to a revelation of cerebral needs. I've done the same in bed with girls. One of the fantasies I've often used is; 'Look there are six men at the bottom of the bed with enormous cocks. They are going to come, but I don't want you to look at their faces. They are watching you now. One has ejaculated and there is spunk on your foot.'

One of my favourite fantasies is anonymity. The fantasy of going to a party where there is a curtain stretched across a room.

Through it, all you can see is the girls' vulvas and thighs, but not their faces. You go up to the curtain, you smell the girls and kiss them, then decide which girl you want to go to bed with. But their only identification is a number on their thighs. Then there is another fantasy where all you choose by is their faces, and another where you choose the woman by just seeing their breasts. In all cases you never really know which woman you went to bed with — just their number. Then there is another fantasy — where you pick up a hitchhiker. It's the anonymity which gives you an escape clause. In sex fantasies no-one wants to feel trapped — you want the eroticism without the relationship — that creates the turn on — the relationship can kill the sex.

If I had to advise a woman on being good in bed I would tell her NOT to act out what she believes to be a role acceptable to her partner or to society. Especially if it doesn't tally with her own individual needs at that time. I would tell her to believe in herself. To love herself. To accept all the sexual attributes that she has. To learn to masturbate. To know her own body, and to be able to look at her vulva in the mirror and not be frightened. To learn to give.

A woman should also be sufficiently discriminating in her partners, so she doesn't go to bed with anybody she doesn't like, because that will create a sense of rejection and disillusionment. She will also encounter bad experiences, which will then re-inforce a bad self-image. A woman should be able to strike a happy medium, so that she doesn't react by discriminating too much; if she is too discriminating she will just price herself out of the market'. She should make her judgement at that particular moment in time with the only rules — those based on experience.

The other day, a girl in her early twenties summed up the whole sexual attitude which I regard as being desirable in a woman. She said; 'I am not married, and if I like a man I am able to go to bed with him — but I am also able not to go to bed with anyone for six months.' She had the freedom to excercise discrimination without feeling pressured into saying 'no' or pressured into saying 'yes'. If a woman likes a man and the input is right and the circumstances are right, she should go to bed with him — if that is what she really wants. She should be free from rules. And I believe that a woman should go to bed with not just who she loves, but also with who she fancies.

XAVIERA HOLLANDER

Ex-New York madam, sex magazine columnist, and best
selling authoress of 'The Happy Hooker' — Xaviera Hollander
is the ultimate media personality. We met at nine on a
Sunday morning in her Left bank Paris hotel and Xaviera
— smaller than I had expected, in blue jeans and an Indian
top, was already programmed for the interview. First though,
she apologised for not wearing any make-up; ('But here is a
photograph of me *with* make-up, taken last week'), and then
invited me to see her appear on a French T.V. show the
following week. Xaviera had been in Paris promoting her new
book; 'Supersex' and was just leaving for the airport, so we
started the interview en route for Charles de Gaulle airport,
and finished it standing in the Air France check-in counter
queue, surrounded by children, old ladies and barking dogs.
Even under those circumstances, Xaviera was extremely
fluent, articulate and unhesitating, answering question after
question confidently, with anecdote after anecdote, produced from what I visualised as a large filing cabinet lodged
somewhere in Xaviera's business-like brain.

When I was a Madam, I chose my girls at orgies or nudist camps.
The girls there obviously enjoyed sex — so I would approach them
and say; 'What's a nice girl like you doing in a place like this when
you could be working in my house and making money.' The girls
I chose had to have fairly good bodies — not flabby, not too
skinny, not too fat, and with no stretch marks. Although I did
have some girls working for me who *were* very skinny or very fat,
because there were always those men who like extremes.

I operated very differently from the French Madam, Madam
Claude — her girls are like dolls. She sends them all to the same
hairdresser, they all have Louis Vuitton handbags and Gucci shoes.
My girls weren't like that at all — they were dressed fairly nicely,
but there were also some girls who looked like real little whores —
because that is what some men really wanted. The girls who had
long legs and nice asses were most in demand — so the short girls
had to work more with their personalities than with their bodies.
And the girls who were most appreciated were always the girls
who were happy and optimistic and knew how to chat to the
clients. But then a man who pays for sex — who goes to a massage

parlour or a whore-house — will always come back, because he is paying for *variety*. What makes a woman good in bed for a whore-house customer is a different girl each time. . .

I have had my best love affairs with women. I prefer men physically — and women emotionally. But with a woman a cock is always missing — and I love cock (my favourite position is 69). From a lesbian point of view though, I prefer a woman who has got personality — even though she may not be too elegant or pretty. Very few women turn me on — because most of them are not at all spontaneous. It is very difficult to find a natural, spontaneous woman. Models, for example, are supposed to be fantastic in bed, but to me they are most boring sexually. I like a woman who can play a masculine and a feminine role in bed.

Brazilian and French women are best in bed. Brazilian women are so sexual that they work men to pieces — their eyes and their bodies seem to ooze sexuality. French women are very bisexual — more than the women of any other race. And I think that the French are the horniest race in the world. Nordics and Swedish women have the reputation of being very hot — they are not really that hot and they don't like to suck off very much. I like English girls because there is something almost pure about them. I've slept with a few English girls — they aren't obviously kinky — but they can be, when they get really turned on.

Jewish girls are the least up-tight women in bed, and Catholic girls are the most uptight. American women are tough bitches in bed. Spanish, Italian and Greek women are absolutely ugly and asexual — in Greece I didn't meet one pretty woman. I've had a few Israeli women. They call them Sabra — Sabra means hard outside and soft inside — but I've yet to meet a Sabra who is soft inside. The ones I went to bed with went through the movements, but were really faking all the time. If a woman isn't wet, if her body doesn't quiver, if her clitoris doesn't throb in my mouth — then I can tell that the woman is faking.

It's easier to fake with a man — and I think 100 percent of women have to be actresses at some time and the man need never know if the woman has really had an orgasm or not. This may be a very anti-woman's lib. statement, but I think a woman should make a man feel like a king — in bed and out of it. I think a woman should compliment a man, give him little tokens of her appreciation. She should please a man emotionally, should make him feel wanted, and be interested in his job. If he is a lawyer or an accountant, she should read up on his profession and not be bored by it.

I think that a good lover always starts with mental stimulation — the head job before the bed job. . . The other day I was in bed with a new friend — an Englishman — and I began talking to him. Usually if I say to a man, 'Do it to me from behind' or 'Slap me on my ass' — and he laughs or gets turned off, I know he is not interested. This Englishman was very shocked, because a woman had never talked dirty to him before. But he got so turned on by it afterwards that he gave me a great fuck. He told me that most women just say, 'Put it in' or 'I'm coming' and have a very short text.

Being sexy and good in bed is inherited. When my grandmother was 86, she was still trying to marry a man who was 20 years younger. My father is a very kinky, very sexy man, but my mother is a very strict (though charming) woman. I inherited everything from my father, because I've got nothing of the pride and coolness of my mother. If I like a man I'm 'on'.

I've never been afraid to ask for what I wanted in bed. I'm so honest — and that might sometimes turn a man off. Sometimes I feel very masochistic and sometimes I feel I really want to get beaten, want to get whipped. I once asked my husband to give me a good spanking and he said, 'I could never hurt you. I love you too much and I'm afraid that once I started it would turn into a very kinky scene.' I didn't push him any further, because I knew he didn't want to. So sometimes he did fuck me roughly, but usually he was very tender with me — which mostly pleased me. If I ever felt like being tied down or beaten I would go to another man who did it to me. I've never felt like beating my husband though, but sometimes when I am with another man, I feel the urge to tie him down and beat him — but I can't do that either — so sometimes you just have to restrict those feelings.

I've never been frigid in my life — except once with my husband. I was wearing a new dress — which make me look very slim. I stood in front of him — rather cockeyed, as if to say, 'I've got a new dress on — doesn't it make me look good?'. I was still waiting for a compliment, when all of a sudden he said, 'What are you waiting for — what's underneath is fat and ugly anyway.' A few minutes later he forgot what he had said, didn't know how he had hurt me — and tried to grab me. I wouldn't let him. I screamed out, 'Don't you touch me — and take that mirror off the ceiling above the bed. I don't want to look at two fat women — myself and my reflection.' I was a stone overweight — and I didn't have an orgasm for three weeks, until I lost that stone. I didn't feel sexy. I just kept telling myself that I was fat and ugly. I felt awful. I couldn't go to bed with a man. I became absolutely frigid. I couldn't have an orgasm. I couldn't even masturbate. I felt like half a woman.

Sometimes I feel as if I am on stage. Once I went to bed with a man I didn't really care about. Stupidly I wanted to prove myself — it was an ego-trip. He was an older man and told me how he read all my books and how he admired me. He took me out to dinner, spent a lot of money on me, and afterwards I really did everything to turn him on, so that he was flabbergasted. But really I was doing the prostitute bit in a different way — saying thank you for the meal. Which is stupid, as I don't have to.

Another time a man I didn't fancy went to bed with me and expected a lot. He asked me to do a 'trip around the world' (eat his ass) — and I couldn't. I felt like puking. The man said, 'But you are the great sex symbol of the seventies. You should do everything — suck my toes — everything.' I said, 'Forget it — I don't even want to be in bed with you. I am not doing this as a prostitute — I am doing you a favour going to bed with you.'

Men are sometimes totally intimidated by going to bed with me and turn temporaily impotent, especially young men because they think, 'She's so experienced — I hope I am good enough for her.' So I say, 'Forget about how many other men I've slept with. No-body has got to prove anything to anybody — I don't have the body of a girl of 18 — neither of us have to prove anything'. A woman should never castrate a man sexually. If he can't get an erection or suffers from premature ejaculation, she should never say something like, 'You are a lousy fuck'. She should coax him gently, so that if he doesn't suck her nipples — she guides his head. If he squeezes her tits too hard, she should take his hands gently.

Above all, no woman should ever have to refuse a man sex — even if she feels ill. Because as long as a woman has a mouth, as long as she can masturbate a man in her hands, or between her tits, he should always be able to have sex with her and she should never have to say no to sex.

CALL GIRL

> Biba, a 'high class' call girl in her thirties, operates from a Beverly Hills appartment. Petite, red-headed, animated exageratedly elegant, Biba looks very like Jane Fonda in 'Klute'.

I like sex, and you have to like sex to be good in bed. I have fun, and I have orgasms with the guys I see professionally. When a new guy walks through this door, it's really exciting and interesting for me because I wonder what his trip is going to be — what he's going to ask me to do. Men expect all kinds of things, and I have some very interesting clients. Helping live out their fantasies and being adaptive to clients is one of the things that make me good in bed. A guy feels safe about telling a professional his fantasies. He is paying for special treatment he can't get from his wife or his girlfriend, so he tells a call girl what he wants her to do.

I see this one guy who is a very famous tennis player, very handsome, and really sweet. But he told me that he couldn't ask his girlfriends to do what he asks me because they would reject him or laugh at him. So when he sees me, he wants me to tie him up; the room has to be dark, I can't talk, there can't be any music. You see, he has a leg and foot fetish. I just lie on the bed and I rub my legs on his cheek and he strokes my legs with his hands very, very gently. His eyes are closed and he is just tripping, and if I put my foot in his face, he has an orgasm. The first time I did that to him, tears were streaming down his face, he was so happy.

I have another client who is a stockbroker and looks like a sweet, all-American boy next door. When he comes here, he likes to crawl on his hands and knees. Then I tie a cord around his cock and lead him around the floor. I wear either boots or black high-heel shoes, my black fishnet stockings, and a lacy black bra. Then I order him to lick my shoes, lick my toes, lick my feet. He loves that. He loves me to sit on his face and smother him with my buttocks. He won't even let me brace myself, and I have to put all my weight on his face. That is not hard work. If I want him to fuck me, then I have him fuck me. If I want him to jack off, then I have him jack off — I order him to. Everything is all right so long as I *order* him to do it.

Other guys like me to pretend to be a little girl. One guy had me fly to Sacramento, and I had to wear a little dress and white cotton panties underneath. He told me about his first sexual experience, which he had when he and the girl were very young. He was reliving the experience.

Some guys I see have incest fantasies. There's an older man I see. He likes me to act the little girl, and I call him Uncle Jack and he loves it. He calls me on the phone from his Rolls Royce when he's driving down the road and he says, 'This is your Uncle Jack. Can I come up and see you?'

I really adapt to the needs of my clients. I care very much about giving them satisfaction so they will come back really happy. I am never judgmental. I never put them down for their fantasies. Sometimes though, it's difficult. I have very few inhibitions left, but once a doctor from Philadelphia offered me a lot of money because he wanted me to pee on him. I was very inhibited about that, but because I am a professional I knew I *had* to do it. So I told the guy to bring me a bottle of champagne, because I needed to be a little bit drunk to be loosened up and able to do it.

But most guys are not that way-out. They want you to pay attention to them, chat to them. They want to have a pretty girl talking to them. They always sense whether the attraction is real or not. You see, I never bullshit clients, I just show them real appreciation, because I really am pleased to see them and I really do enjoy them in bed. So I don't have to say, 'Oh you are fantastic,' (unless the guy hints that he wants that).

There's a producer I see who told me he met some girl who said his cock was so big and tasted so good. His cock really is just average, but I realized, by what he said, that he needed to be told differently. So if that's what he wants, then that's what I do, and I tell him, 'Oh, she was certainly right.' Usually, though, I talk very little to my clients in bed, and I don't talk dirty unless the guy asks for it. Otherwise, I am very much the lady in every sense, and I never swear.

I started out by working for Dixie, a madam, and she taught me a lot, and 'turned me out'. When we met, we just talked and she told me to lose weight, which I did. She also told me not to wear wigs, only to wear real gold jewelry, not tons of make-up, and no false eyelashes. Also, she told me to wear a light perfume and long dresses which look elegant and classy, and are easy to get in and out of − long dresses that you don't have to wear anything underneath.

Dixie didn't tell me anything about technique, but she explained how to cope if a guy gets too rough — you act really sweet and calm. But, anyway, when you work for a madam you have protection, because she is in the other room and the guys know that you can always call her. The only trouble is that a couple of guys have wanted to fuck me really really hard, so I just say, 'Honey, not so hard. I'm just a little thing,' or else, 'Oh, honey, your cock's so big it's hurting me' in a little tiny voice. Dixie told me that when that happens, I should wrap my legs around the man's back and brace myself with my thighs, so even though the guy is really banging on your thigh and not your pussy, he thinks you have wrapped your legs around him to pull him closer to you.

I don't like my tricks to fuck me really hard, but my boyfriend always fucks me really, really hard, and I like that. I keep a real definite separation between my lovers and my tricks. When I'm with my boyfriend in bed, we look in each other's eyes while we make love. I love that. It increases the intensity of the experience. I don't do that with my clients. I don't look into their eyes because I don't want that closeness with a client. My boyfriend and I act out my fantasies. I have masochistic fantasies, and I only act them out with him. Sometimes I have a little bruise on my arm or on my leg, and then the guys who see me professionally say, 'Oh, Biba, who did that to you? Oh, how terrible?' and they get really upset.

A lot of guys who see me for business spend all their time eating me. They say, 'Biba, if I can make you come, that's important for me.' I think eating a woman is the nicest thing a guy can do. I get a customer who comes from San Diego every Friday and brings a little brown bag of all the things he wants to eat out of my pussy: bananas, whipped cream, chocolate-covered cherries and strawberries. When he does that, I have fun; having fun is one of the most important things about being good in bed.

Giving head matters a lot in bed, and also phallic worship. When I am with my Uncle Jack (as the little girl) and we neck for a while on the couch, then I have him unzip his fly and get his cock out, and I get down on my knees and I take his cock and rub it over my cheeks and over my lips and over my eyes. It's like worshipping it; then he knows that I really appreciate it and it's not just a quick blowjob. I swallow a man's come if I know the guy and he doesn't taste bad. Every guy tastes so different. I'm sure women also taste differently as well.

I am just getting better and better in bed. Guys teach me different things, and I have plenty of time and opportunity to experiment. If a woman asked how to be good in bed, I would advise her to ask her man to tell her his fantasy. If she found it difficult to ask, I would advise her to say, 'Is there any special way I can please you? What would you like? I'll do anything. Just ask me and I'll do it.'

You should also experiment with a guy's body and how he feels good, and you should change positions with him. You should also get in touch with your own fantasies and your own trips and not be so concerned about just pleasing the man. Allow him to please you too. Both of you should share your fantasies and what turns you on, then you will both be satisfied. It's not a one-way deal. You should also make love in different kinds of places. I like to do something very trippy. I might make love in front of a mirror, or do it in front of the fireplace, or on the diningroom table.

Guys turn on to a woman if she's sweet, feminine, sexy, and really interested in him. (It doesn't matter what she really looks like). And a woman who wants to be good in bed should never judge the man she is in bed with. In this business I have learned that sex is a very individual thing, that each person wants something different and *is* something different. It doesn't matter what the guy looks like. He can be big and fat, or real old, or real skinny. None of that matters. I suspend all judgments. I just enjoy the men's warmth and just being close to them.

EX-PIMP: ICEBERG SLIM

Although I have fantasised about being a call-girl like Biba — none of my fantasies ever included having a pimp. When I read black ex-pimp Iceberg Slim's memoirs: *Pimp*, I knew my instincts had been right. The book describes Iceberg's life as pimp for over 500 women and of his 'stable' where the girls ('bitches') often died of abortions. Meanwhile, as befitted a pimp, Iceberg just 'rested and dressed' and drove around in his Cadillac, traditionally a pimp's pride, joy and trademark. In California where cars can be registered with names, I once saw a pimp's cadillac displaying the number-plate; PAY ME.

But until Iceberg Slim (real name Bob Beck), I had never actually met a genuine pimp. Iceberg, retired now, lives in Los Angeles with his wife and four children. When I phoned him, his wife answered — then Iceberg came to the phone and in a very deep voice, said; 'This is Slim — Iceberg Slim — who are you?'. I shivered, hovering between feeling sexual and afraid, hesitated, then arranged the interview. When we met at his Spanish style house, Iceberg, in his fifties, wore white trousers, a blue silk shirt, with his hair carefully arranged on his forehead in large, shining, black curls. His eyes were very piercing and I felt that although his days of pimping were long past, Iceberg relished resuscitating the old mood, creating the old effect and would have enjoyed frightening me.

I could never tell if a woman was going to be good in bed until she performed with me. I've known whores who were the ultimate projection of exciting sex, only to discover that they were *not* good in bed. I could never go on assumptions about a whore's performance in bed, because she might end up not making money, which would lead to the worst possible confrontation: between a pimp and a job.

Pimps are asexual. I was in it for the money and not the sex. When you have a stable of twenty girls working for you, you are in trouble if you are into being a superstud. Career pimps, as I was, try to preserve themselves, to conserve their energy. I always appeared very sour, otherwise whores got you in the end. When a pimp was hooked on a whore, we would say, 'He has got that bitch's scent up his nose.' The essence of the woman got tied up inside their brains, weakening them.

But whores are better in bed than most women. The sexual peak is prior to menopause for most women, the golden age for a woman to be good in bed. But that age is less marketable than youth. Whores are good for acrobatics and slavish devotion — they make the best mechanics. When I say slavish devotion, a whore won't *really* do anything, but she still leaves you with the impression that she has done everything — because whores use their hands, their feet, their voices — they are like quicksilver. They needed to be, because my whores worked eighteen hours a day, and had to bring back $100 a day, even in the thirties.

I like a woman to come to me bringing a reputation for wicked eroticism. Not that she is a pushover, but that she is always free (unlike a whore) to choose whoever she goes to bed with, and that no one forces her or owns her. There is a kind of choreography of sex that matters. Some women, after they have had sex with you for about the third time, have the aptitude to mesh with you. Everything is fluid as you move her through the various sexual positions with the pressure of your fingertips, or even the voice. She flows with you.

Erotic tastebuds also make a woman good in bed, when a woman knows what you want without being told, almost by witchcraft. Also, power in bed is very important: a crossbow back, lots of strength, so that you know when you have taken her to the peak, it will be drama the moment you push her off.

I don't think a woman is less good in bed if she takes a long time to come. I am suspicious of a woman whose furnace you can set ablaze immediately, because sometimes she is faking, or is a nymphomaniac and then you can never hope to satisfy her. Some women are very silent in bed, but I think that the best women are always those who carry on an erotic conversation, a reportage of of what they are doing while you are in bed. That is important for the man who really considers himself a great lover, because the woman heightens his glorious self-image by reporting along the way. A woman can also create a good self-image for herself by thinking of herself as an assassin, a killer in bed, with the destruction of the man her ultimate goal.

I've never forced a woman to do anything in bed. Women always did what I wanted anyway – they were all good partners and wanted to please me. I am not talking about whores – they try to tire pimps out with fellatio. They do it all the time, even in the car – and they swallow (it kills oral sex if a woman refuses to swallow).

Physical build doesn't make a woman better in bed, just different. Thin women are more susceptible to choreography, more fluidity, but plump women also compete in their own way, with warmth and softness. Chemistry has a lot to do with what makes a woman good in bed. It is produced when two psyches meet and their oils, their fluids, coalesce; that is what produces good sex.

MALE PROSTITUTE

Male prostitution for women is becoming popular in California and Las Vegas; the 'Las Vegas Panorama' newspaper advertises; 'male escorts', the Las Vegas police department licences the agencies and each male prostitute is subject to regular medical inspections. Las Vegas male prostitutes charge women from $70 an hour and expect to be tipped. In Las Vegas, vice capital of America, I talked to a male prostitute who told me that he serviced four women a day. Although the men are officially described as 'escorts' I learned that women hired them specifically for sex. The women were sometimes in their twenties, and didn't want to risk picking up a man, especially in crime-ridden Las Vegas. Other customers were famous women, or wives of famous men, seeking sex and discretion. Other women wanted to buy sexual experimentation, as they were unwilling to experiment with a man they loved. Fathers occasionally even hired a male prostitute to 'devirginise' their daughters professionally. The ex-prostitute I interviewed, Michael Kearns, slept with over 350 women during his short career. He is tall, muscular, in his late twenties — and looks extremely fresh-faced and boyish.

Women are made to feel insecure because there are all sorts of silly platitudes about what makes a woman good in bed. If I averaged out the best sexual experiences, they weren't with women who are blond and twenty. The ideal woman in bed can be anything physically — not always thin or fat, not always tall or small. I can tell how highly sexed a woman is by watching her eat — the sensuousness of holding a glass shows if the woman is good, if she handles it as if she was handling a cock. You get a whole feeling of rhythm, which is important; I can sometimes even tell if a woman is good on the phone by the rhythm, the intensity of a woman's voice.

I can always tell if a woman is good in bed by looking into her eyes, or at her mouth. I really think eyes and mouths have a lot to do with being good in bed. Marilyn Monroe looked as if she was very good — she had the right mouth — but I never went to bed with her, so I am not certain. Perhaps she wasn't good at all, just because she projected it so strongly. The projection of sex often means that the woman can be a flop in bed. There are so many sex goddesses who have flopped in the bedroom, so instead, they have sex with the whole world.

I don't think a woman is very good in bed if she *thinks* about being good while she is having sex. There has to be some spontaneity. The inhibitions do lessen after a certain amount of experience, or when a woman gets involved in an emotional attachment which makes her feel free and uninhibited. The ideal sexual situation is the freedom to do whatever you want in bed.

A lot of women come to me because they have insecurities, the worst being oral sex; at thirty-five they are doing it for the first time. (Some people, even today, still think that sex exists just to have children.) Other women were housewives and used my services because they wanted something different and were afraid to ask for it. Demands need to be made in bed, but a lot of women don't know how to make demands — they are so scared of not being thought good.

I am really a feminist. I think the woman has felt at a gut level that she should not have a sexual self or explore. Women's idea of sex used to be passive and to do whatever the man asks. I disagree with that. On any level, not just physical, it is pointless to have a relationship with someone who only wants to please you. What I would like to say to all women is, 'Get rid of stereotypes, forget all that masculine and feminine labelling.' I am not saying that we should reverse roles, but that each individual has the capacity to relate or interelate in many different ways — some masculine and some feminine. I don't think that softness in a man should be despised, or toughness in a woman condemned.

I like older women, assertive women — not that I like whips and chains, but I do like a woman who does what she wants in bed. I think what makes a woman good is being able to give and take — she should never be just the giver.

Of course, there are some women who are bad in bed because they are scared and they are very submissive, or they are lazy and don't move. It's easy to just lie there. But a woman isn't bad if she takes a long time to come. Some men keep asking if the woman has come, but that acts like a stop-light to women; it makes them freeze.

I don't try to judge my partner or say, 'Did you come?' or 'You were really good.' I don't verbalize in bed. But, at the same time,

I would never pretend I am the perfect screw, or that because I am six-foot-two, I might be better than someone who is five-foot-two. Society has shoved down our throats everything that we are supposed to be so that you feel that if you don't look like someone in a commercial, you shouldn't have sex.

The trouble is that everyone is scared — and sexually scared of not being perfect, but no one is perfect in bed; everyone is different — sexually, emotionally, intellectually, physically. No matter how similar we may *seem*, there is always something different. Everyone should hold fast to that. Every single woman I have been with has been totally different in bed. We are not only different from one another, we are also totally different from moment to moment, from day to day, from hour to hour. In the course of intercourse, our moods change, our fantasies change. No two people are alike. There is no good in bed, or bad in bed, just different.

'Swinging Sixties'

MANDY RICE DAVIES

Mandy Rice Davies, who now lives in Tel Aviv, was in New
York for only two days, appearing in an Israeli film. She
was unable to see me — but we talked over the phone. Mandy
was very chatty and laughed a lot — particularly when I
told her that I remembered reading the Profumo trial reports
secretly, when I was ten.

I have faked in bed, and the men were absolutely, completely
convinced by my faking. My secret is *not* to make a lot of noise,
to be a good actress, and never, never overact. Enjoying sex is
being good in bed, but I should think 80 percent of women fake
to give the appearance of being good in bed. A woman can be
good, in a man's view, yet not enjoy sex — except that never
works in the long run. You can fake on a one-night stand, but not
in a relationship carried over the years. I don't think women are
born good in bed. All that comes later — usually much later in life
— if they havn't been spoiled already by faking and not being
honest.

If a woman wanted to project her 'good in bed' quality, I would
always advise her to look non-sexy. Low-cut dresses seem out of
date, and looking sexy is a very low-class turn on. I don't think
men are turned on in the flesh by overt sex. It is important to be
a little more cool if you want to attract a glamorous man. The
exploding iceberg bit works far better than looking sexy does. I
also think charm is important; charm is the biggest aphrodisiac in
the world. But you can't really define it, because some people just
are awfully charming because of their smiles, their manners, and
their warmth.

Mystery matters in bed. I don't agree with talking a lot in bed,
and I don't use words to turn a man on, although it is important
for a woman to be able to ask for what she wants in bed. She
should always wait for the right opportunity though. For example,
it is easier to make sexual demands on those evenings when two
people are very turned on and are at an ideal point in their
relationship. But when a woman meets a man for the first time,
she should never make demands.

I'm for anything that is basically between two people; as far
as oral sex is concerned, I'm in. But I wouldn't like a guy who
suggested orgies or threesomes in bed. If I were in love with him,

I would probably fall out of love with him immediately. I fall in love with someone I have something in common with; I'm way past the age of falling in love with a man for mysterious reasons. And I am not really interested in anything beyond what happens between two people in bed.

I don't really think the average person wants to cross certain lines, sexually. People still like sexual secrecy. In a magazine there was a cartoon of group sex. Two people were screwing, and the man was saying, 'I'll tell my wife I'm working late,' and the woman says, 'I'll tell my husband I'm going to the movies.' In the middle of an orgy where they both could screw quite freely, they still wanted to have secret meetings.

I am not interested in group sex. Once, though, I was invited to a party which turned out to be the only orgy I've ever been to in my life. Somebody answered the door in his socks. I thought it was a joke and said, 'Don't be silly. Put your clothes on.' I was embarrassed to admit that I didn't like it. Anyway, recently the girl that gave the orgy wrote an article about me. The orgy was years ago, but I picked up the magazine and read: 'Mandy Rice Davies walked into the orgy, took a look around and walked out, obviously frigid.' I loved that.

Kinky sex just doesn't turn me on. I can assure you there has never been anything like sadomasochism in my relationships. The Profumo Affair, it was – how can I describe it? – naive decadence. At the time, though, you see, it sounded awfully out of place. The affairs were perfectly moral, but what happened around them was a little more decadent. But when scandals start snowballing, they gather up everything around. I had had a brief affair with Lord Astor and Douglas Fairbanks, Jr., but none of those involved anything remotely kinky.

I am not as hot as I was made out. People who are given a sexy image often get inhibited. Men sometimes react to a woman with a sexy image quite differently from what you might expect. Men very often don't want to go to bed with me because they are trying to prove that they don't fancy me, or else that they don't want me just for sex.

I had one or two relationships with male movie stars at the time when I was very well-known. We were both incredibly nervous. *I* was nervous because *he* was supposed to have a reputation for being good in bed, and *he* was nervous because *I* was supposed to have a reputation for being good in bed. So, instead of the sex being very hot and heavy, in the end nothing happened at all and we finished off just sitting in bed having coffee and sandwiches.

JACK NICHOLSON

'What makes a woman G.I.B?' I think feeling makes a woman good in bed. If it's not real, don't do it. I have a background in Reichian therapy, and that's pretty much what it boils down to. If you really don't feel something, don't fake it. Just stop right there, even if it's with your wife, because forced sex is like forced energy of any kind — it doesn't really work. I think that sexuality and sexual expression are really units of energy that are communicable — just like you change the way you feel when somebody just looks at you. I think that the change is a real thing.

JUSTIN DE VILLENEUVE

Justin de Villeneuve — photographer and discoverer of Twiggy — seemed an obvious choice. I couldn't help waiting for allusions to Twiggy from her ex-mentor, but Justin didn't make any. Jan, his beautiful American model-girl wife was very much in evidence, brought tea into the studio where we were doing the interview and said; 'I used to be blonde — so if he says he likes blondes — he means me as well.' Justin told me he had already worked out what he was going to say — stared at me very intently, cracked a few jokes, spoke slowly and softly and was less flashy than I had expected.

I used to look very pretty (I am getting over it now) and I used to be known for having incredible girlfriends. Most of them were models and most of them were useless in bed. Most models are too 'into' themselves, and they are stupid. I used to have a very beautiful girlfriend who was useless — just lay in bed like a big lump of dough. Then there was another young girl of sixteen, 5'.11", long legs and the most incredible body I have ever seen — Very tall, big bust — beautiful. But she was just stupid and it all came out in bed. I was in the middle of getting my act together

51

in bed and she suddenly started talking about the car. I used to drive very fast and she'd say 'Were you doing 100 m.p.h. when you passed that car?' or 'Did you park the car safely?' It was over very quickly because she was stupid — she was bad in bed because her mind wasn't there.

I just have to talk to a woman for five minutes and I can tell if she's going to be good in bed. I think there is a tie-up between intelligence and a woman being good in bed. I've got the feeling that intellectual career girls are better in bed. Sometimes, though, you get the ones that are a bit heavy — that think far too much — like the Women's Lib. ladies. I think they feel insecure so they hide behind Women's Lib. — I find most of them are very boring and unattractive anyway.

I get turned on by a lot of girls. Most of my women have been tall — but you can have short, big girls who are wonderful as well. A beautiful girl can be awful and you can have a very plain girl who is very passionate, screams and shouts in bed, seems to really enjoy it — wonderful. I can go into an office and fall in love with a secretary who is probably very plain and wouldn't know that I fancied her.

The other day there was a parking lady in Tottenham Court Road who was gorgeous — black stockings and a yellow hat. I had wonderful fantasies about her. I told her I was in love with her and she said, 'Don't be silly.' And I saw a policewoman in the city the other day. She had flat shoes on, big shoulders, lovely face, her hair pulled back — she was wonderful, much more attractive than a model.

I am married now — but I used to fall in love very easily. I'd think I was in love and send flowers and do the whole de Villeneuve number. Then after a while I was nearly always disappointed and I'd think — 'What did I send flowers for?' I get turned-off if girls get too possessive. Sex has got to be fun. I think that funny girls are best in bed. If they are serious — they usually get serious within the relationship — then it doesn't work.

I like to think that love makes sex specially good — but it doesn't. One of the best sexual relationships I've had was with a very ambitious, very beautiful French model. I met her at 'Harper's Bazaar' — she was in England for a few days and her father was Canadian — an ambassador in France. We caught each other's eye — and ten minutes later we were back at my studio. I don't ever do that so quickly — I usually take weeks before I go to bed with a girl.

I was nervous — and the problem was mine not hers — I am very nervous myself — the first time — you feel you're being tested and I think a woman also feels the same. So the first time is not really good. Anyway — with this girl it was a bit embarrassing — so I said 'Let's go to Tramp'. We did — and when we were dancing it felt so good that I said 'I think we should go back home again'. We did — and it was wonderful. I really liked her — she really liked me — she was incredible and it just worked. Lot's of fun, lot's of laughing — she stayed with me for two days and I never saw her again. She just wanted to enjoy sex — there was certainly no love — it was purely sex — but it was wonderful.

Usually — if I've known a girl for a long time then everything is permissible for me. Say I've had a relationship for a month — then I feel everything is okay. Some girls are pushy and I find them intimidating until I know them. But if a girl refuses something I want in bed it doesn't turn me off but just makes me try harder.

I don't think a woman is less good if it takes her a long time to come. Some men, I understand, are rather selfish, but part of it for me is that the woman enjoys it. I try hard to make the woman have an orgasm without making it *obvious* that I am trying. I suppose a girl could make out that she had come anyway — but it's a bit off-putting. I really think that if a woman feels insecure it's the man's fault. I believe there should still be romance and lots of hugging and kissing until a girl leaves the front door.

I feel insecure if a girl asks for what she wants in bed. I was in the South of France and there was this beautiful girl. She was there for the premier of a film at the Cannes Film Festival and she got great reviews — but I can't say who she was because she's very well known. When I met her I did a bit of a de Villeneuve chat-up. I was staying at an apartment and I cancelled her hotel and found the most beautiful hotel overlooking the sea at Cannes — little green shutters — so romantic. We had dinner — wine — I had a tan — my white suit on — I was very suave. We went back to the hotel and it was so romantic — like a honeymoon. If we had made love immediately it would have been perfect but before we started she said something that really put me off: 'When I saw you I really wanted to fuck you'. It was crude, the way she said it — I had a terrible mental block and I just couldn't do it. And it all ended up

53

a bit embarrassing because I couldn't do it. The girl turned round and said 'Are you homosexual?' So I said 'Well – don't tell anyone – I have a problem. . .' I didn't want her to lose face so I had to make out I was homosexual without really admitting it. I didn't want to upset her – she's so lovely, I really like her, it's just that words can put me off.

There was another time I had a romance with an American girl. We had a romance for three months, met in L.A., but didn't consummate the romance. Then one day I did the deed, it worked out and I quite enjoyed it. Afterwards we went downstairs without any clothes on to this huge Bedouin tent I've got in my studio. And she said – 'Where's your pisser?' – I went 'There' – but it was over for me. After three months of phone calls to America – of building up this romance – it was over. She might have been breathtakingly beautiful, she might have been tall and statuesque, she might have been good in bed, but as soon as she said that it was over because words are so important to me.

MICHAEL CAINE

'What makes a woman G.I.B?' It has nothing to do with beauty. There is no way you can tell by looking at her.

VICKI HODGE

I met model Vicki Hodge over lunch in Chelsea, while I was interviewing Angie Bowie. I told Vicki about my book and asked for an interview. She opened her eyes very widely and said she would love to be interviewed. So she was, at her house in Fulham, where we had tea in Vicki's bedroom, which smelt of incence. Her boyfriend John joined us, Vicki was full of enthusiasm, giggling – true to her sexy image. But later, she exhibited another facet. I mentioned that I was about to promote the G.I.B. book in America and Vicki told me that she had also toured the States, promoting 'Birds of Britain' – 'they will try and send you up and treat you like a dizzy dolly bird. But always remember to be very British and professional and proud of your book' – so revealing the shrewd professional behind the pin-up façade.

I know I am a good fuck. All my men have stayed with me for a long time. I was always very sexual with them — so they weren't just saying goodbye to me, they were also saying goodbye to a good lover. I assess my sexual capabilities on the fact that I've got an old man who is highly desirable and desired. I've been with him for eight years, yet I can still keep him happy in bed for weeks. John and I can fuck fifteen times a day and we often fuck seven times a night. I am basically very straight, but I think I need a lot of fucking. John has fucked me up walls, in lifts, in people's kitchens, in trains, while standing at a wedding reception — wherever he wants to. That to me is outrageous — I just love it.

I never worry that another woman John may fuck might be better in bed. I have total confidence in my body and in my capabilities. I know my body is like the ideal fantasy lover. I've heard ex-lovers talk about me twelve years later and they say, 'She was an amazing fuck, she's got a body like a piece of elastic.' I am completely double-jointed — I can do any position. I'm an amazingly sexy dancer and I can do everything I do on the dance floor laying down with someone else, in front, behind, with my back arched like a 'U'. I'll do anything. Any position.

I think I was born liking sex, I'm a terribly earthy person. I am country bred and I've seen cows fucking since I was two. I lost my virginity when I was nine years old doing the splits. I used to masturbate at school but I think it was probably more like a mental turn-on.

I knew I was turning men on at twelve — and I first had a fuck at thirteen. By the time I was nineteen I had already been to bed with ten men. I nearly married one of them — a very straight guy — who made me pregnant and by whom I had three abortions. I didn't know anything about sex, I'd never given head, and I'd never ever had an orgasm. Then, at nineteen, I went out with a pop singer. He taught me how to fuck, how to come, how to feel, and how to give head. When he had a drink he used to suffer from the 'dreaded droop'. So I learned about giving head, I didn't particularly like it, but it had amazing results within seconds.

I learned to be good. I learned how to hold a man's penis — how gently you have to hold it — that it's not just a cock that's got to be made hard and put inside you. It has got to be handled and loved, and stroked and cuddled and kissed. I never realised how sensitive a man is between his legs, as sensitive as a woman. And how you can arouse him just by touching him. And I learned to have orgasms. I had been fucking this other guy with a needle dick for years and thinking 'My God I must read more books because I've never had orgasms.' And I don't think anybody is good in bed until they have had an orgasm.

I had an eight or nine month period of stray fucks. There were some men who just went round fucking and never saw you again. But I've never felt bad in bed. Of course there's nothing like first night nerves, but I've never been to bed with a man who hasn't had an orgasm. I've always gone out of the way to do my bit — which is not just going 'Ooh, groovy, fantastic' and not doing anything else.

I've been to bed with a woman — but I really didn't get much out of it — I just wanted to give it a go in case I was missing something. But I wasn't. One thing I have never done is being fucked up the arse. I couldn't do it, not even finger up. It always makes me think of dirt. I'm also frightened to. Anyway it's impossible with John because he's too big. I've also never seen two people fuck — the idea doesn't turn me on. I make pale blue movies (they go on general release) but I don't get my rocks off that way. I make movies about fucking, because I earn a lot of money and because I'm good at it. I'm always naked, my legs are in places where people shouldn't have legs and I am so supple that audiences say, 'She must be a young chick'. But I have to play the sex down — to a quarter of what I usually do in bed.

Since I've been with John I've always, always come. And I've never ever refused him anything he wanted in bed. A woman should never refuse a man because if you do you belittle him more than if you cut his balls off. If you ever undermine a man, if you ever make a man lose an ounce of his pride then you're playing games. You are playing with fire. Because a man is like a piece of porcelain — if you start chipping away you will hurt him inside. And he functions from inside, he goes hard from inside — so if he thinks you took the piss out of him there is no way in which he will get it on. A woman must never demand sexual equality.

I am totally owned and I love it. I am totally satisfied and I don't need anything else. I've got such a strong relationship with John that fucking is secondary. Before John it was always getting over the fuck and into the relationship. But I still think sex plays an amazingly important part in a relationship. Mortgages and bills destroy relationships and if you're not going to bed and fucking you become even more uptight. So if you have a few hours of love, of good fucking in bed, a man can let out a ton of worries and a chick can feel great for days.

Conscience can ruin relationships. There's no one who can swear they are faithful. So they sometimes go off and have a fuck and then they get a conscience. I know a lot of women who have affairs but are still happy with their old men. When they come home afterwards, they won't fuck their old men for four days, because they feel dirty. So that causes terrible rows and damages the relationship. Of course it is more difficult for a chick to have a screw because a man 'comes' into a woman. It's easier for a man — he can stick it in anywhere, into a mousehole if he wants. So if he wants to go off and fuck — great — but he shouldn't let his old lady know.

I have only one rule in my sex games. That is; never ever fuck somebody else's old man without caring. Be cool about it. Don't do it casually. And never, ever hurt anybody because fucking is something you can do with any Tom, Dick or Harry — but loving somebody isn't.

BERNIE CORNFELD

'What makes a woman G.I.B?' A lot of tenderness, I would think.

PATRICK LICHFIELD

I promised Patrick Lichfield that his interview would not be used for serialisation or published in excerpts anywhere other than in this book. His reasons for asking were obvious — it was not difficult to imagine world-wide headlines about 'the Queen of England's cousin' telling all. So I agreed and interviewed Patrick in his Kensington studio; since then he has photographed me for the cover of this book, married Lady Leonora Grosvenor and become the father of a little girl.

This may make me sound extremely ordinary, but I don't think there are any women that I have met who couldn't be reasonably good. The most interesting thing about my love life has been its variety. I never quite reached the point of saturation, even during that time when we were all 'at it', but I did find that I was ringing the changes quite a lot, the women didn't look the same, and none of them was an ideal looking lady. So the first and most important thing is that you can't describe good in bed in terms of looks. I got very spoilt with the availability of women when I was very young — because of my job. I have been confronted all my working life with actresses and models and they aren't any different. Of course they are appealing in the sense that they are decorative and they stand out in a crowd. And since one was a child the kind of woman the cheaper newspapers use as sex symbols have been engrained in one's mind. Illustrative art has very often used a certain shape, a certain type of mouth, to indicate sexual prowess and talent — so one often believes that those kinds of women are going to be marvellous in bed.

That is not always the case. I was a photographer's assistant and I got the last chance at the model in the studio. Everybody always precedes the most junior assistant; the photographer has first go, then the art director, then everybody else. I was talking to a very much more successful photographer than myself and he said, 'Oh, don't ever go for the models for God's sake — go for the girl that brings round the clothes, or go for the hairdresser, or go for the make-up girl, or go for the editor.' That's true because although they invariably will not be SEEN to be attractive, in the obvious sense, they really want to be remembered. Thank goo ' ness people are so very different anyway. Because if everybody did look like little Anne Fanny we'd all be quite satisfied with those awful blow-up robber dolls.

A beautiful woman *can* be very interesting because you do want to turn her on. But I think one of the most exciting things is when you get someone who looks as if she has never seen a man — women who carry a signal on their faces which say, 'I am so goody-goody and holier-than-thou, that I've never seen a man without his clothes on before.' If you can really get her turned on — I think that is the most exciting thing, to turn a woman on — so if you can do that, then you're turned on as well. I find now, funnily enough, that the over-sexy image is a little bit of a downer, an off-putter because everybody can appear sexy. If a woman overdoes it, or overplays it you think, 'Heavens this lady eats young men for breakfast' — it's all show and it's going to be a bore. If you see it coming a mile away you don't try so hard as when you don't expect it and then suddenly get surprised. It is the surprises that are exciting — I suppose memorably the most exciting people in bed were really the people I never expected to go to bed with. The circumstances contrived to enable you to do it. Just two moments — and I'm a rather fatalistic person — it happened, bang!

I never looked at sex as a conquest — I never looked upon it as scoring notches on the butt of one's rifle. I don't want to abuse women and tell them what to do and ill-treat them — that is alien to me. I think it is very important to combine a soothing fondness and an eroticism in bed. You can have one, and you can have the other, but very seldom do you find the two — very rarely in one woman for one person. It's fantastic if, on the erotic side, a woman can be abandoned enough for you to totally forget where you are and what you're doing; to forget that you're grown up, dressed, walking, talking and so on — that's a marvellous moment. And then the other thing is if you do actually feel you're getting as close as possible to that person.

A good man makes a woman good — I think a woman who is not reasonably good is that way because she hasn't been with the right person and because nobody has bothered to take care of her. There may be some women who are natural — who are sensuous. A woman has got to have a sensual side to her nature. It may not be displayed all the time and it may take a little getting out. You can do that before you get anywhere near bed, which is lovely — I find that very exciting. If a woman starts off with the advantage of being sensuous and actually enjoying sex (I don't mean that she's a scrubber and in and out of bed with everybody — some kind of nymph) but that she is actually turned on by sex, then she's going to be improved if she has the care of somebody else who's good and knows what he's doing.

The other thing that makes women good in bed is not having to prove that they are sexually ravenous, or that they have got to be screwed every night, or five times a night, or twelve times a day, or whatever, but are actually able to communicate to you when they really want it and understand when you really want it, and when you don't.

Also I think that women are so good at faking. Quite a lot of the orgasms men think they have caused are probably non-existent. If you really have a relationship where women are honest with you I think one learns some surprising things that make you really think, 'I've been kidded now and again.' I don't think orgasm is the ultimate target.

A woman is enormously helpful if she asks for what she wants in bed. It's lovely, it's absolutely marvellous. You don't pick up a camera without reading the instruction manual first – you want to see what it can do. Provided that she doesn't like something that is either impossibly uncomfortable or continuously wants to do something that is vaguely against your nature or what you would call generally 'unnatural' and provided it isn't something you actually don't like doing. But if you know what turns the woman on it's a winner. It's like putting on the right suit for the girl; it's like wearing the right clothes; it's like her wearing the right dress for you; it's like giving her ice cream or caviar if she likes that. And there is no point in forcing sardines or pilchards down her throat if what she really wants is smoked salmon.

The women to me who aren't good in bed are the women you expect too much of – invariably the idol. In the same way as I would hate to be somebody like Robert Redford – because whatever I did it would be considered ordinary – women would be surprised at how ordinary I probably was. Twenty years ago, if you were totally direct about somebody you'd say, 'Is he rich?' or, 'Is he intelligent?' and these were the status symbols – now the status symbol has changed completely to, 'Is he a good lay?'. I don't believe there is such a thing as a good lay. I once met a man who said, 'I've never been to bed with a lady who hasn't had an orgasm.' I thought he was an absolute liar – but he's probably one of those people that some women say is marvellous and some women say isn't. All I know is that I probably have spent an awful lot of nights with an awful lot of ladies and some of them will have gone away with the thought that I was perfectly awful – but hopefully one or two of them will remember a moment or two of pleasure. It truly, I think, depends so much on the circumstances and the person.

I imagine that you go on learning about sex until you're too old to do it and that everyone with a little bit of encouragement, can be good at it. An awful lot of people go into life groping for experience in groping. And only when they either get married or settle down do they realise that it has taken them all that time to actually be able to press the right buttons. And it is precisely like the man who goes out and buys the fastest motorbike in the world – because he is the richest man in the world – but nobody has ever told him how to lean on a corner, how to brake a little earlier, how to accelerate without getting wheel-spin. But by the time you've given up the motorbike kick, and have actually stopped riding motorbikes, you're bloody good at it.

I shudder to think of my youth and the clumsiness and the sort of rough manhandling that one gave people without any degree of finesse. But I *was* very lucky because I was taught very early on by a lady – who had no business to be interferring with me at the age that she did. I was very young, too young really to enjoy what I was doing. I think I must have been ten and she was the art mistress at the school I was at. She used to make me do things to her and she taught me an awful lot of extremely valuable information which came in useful later in life, not then, because I couldn't put it into practice. And she showed me what buttons to press to turn her on.

The ladies that are sexually memorable are memorable sometimes because of the fact that they were early on in my life and therefore they are engrained in my memory like anything that you do – your first cigarette, your first car – or that they taught me something if I was prepared to learn. One of the most memorable experiences was when I was trying to go out with a lady and I got picked up by her mother. Wrong generation, and yet it was absolutely stunning. In my mind I had created that girl as being the girl of the moment. I was eighteen and she was seventeen and her mother was probably older than I am now. But it was just an astonishingly exciting thing to happen.

I remember being very upset when I was about twenty because I couldn't get near one girl who I fancied no end, because she kept going out with a guy who was about thirty-five or forty. I kept saying to her, 'What the hell do you see in that guy? I mean he's old.' Actually he was as old as I am now. And now I see why she did. Once or twice I came across women who were either terrified, or not turned on. In one instance I remember thinking it must be my fault, and in normal circumstances I would probably have left that as a one night stand. But I didn't. I took her out again and the same thing happened the next night. I happened upon her twelve years later and she turned out to have changed considerably. It was probably because I wasn't good enough at that age anyway.

The most important experiences were when the women contrived to include, or managed somehow to include, a romantic situation during a time in the sixties when in fact romance was so very lacking. You see I was brought up, luckily, just before the sexual revolution took place in the early sixties, a quite extraordinary time. I suppose there were a few of us like Bailey and Bentley who had had to fight for it in our youth, and then were grabbed by older ladies and taught the ropes and then, suddenly, were thrown out on the streets to find that, in fact, everybody was doing it with everybody else and there was no great chase. I mean you could actually get laid, just like that. And it happened very fast. And it was so easy to actually get somebody into bed. I think it is slowing up again now.

But I think that you can always get a woman into bed with a combination of ploys. One high on the list is discretion. Another one is that I really believe very few Englishmen and even less Americans truly like women. And I mean by that *really* like women. If you said to any red-blooded Englishman, 'If you were to go on a desert island what would be one of the things you'd take?' they'd all say 'A woman'. But really, unless they were truly in love with somebody and had that woman in mind, they would rather be on that desert island, or sitting at breakfast or at tea or on a bus or anywhere you like — with a man. Underneath everything, our whole background and upbringing tend to make us much better at dealing with men.

And I have been very lucky and found myself always more easy, more comfortable and generally wholly happier if I am in the company of a woman. I really don't believe that there are enough people who spend time actually trying to like women — with their clothes on as well as without. And I think in order for somebody to be good in bed they've got to be very good out of bed as well. And I wouldn't want to go to bed with a woman if the only time I ever wanted to see her was in bed.

JOHN WAYNE

'What makes a woman G.I.B.?' Being there.

IMOGEN HASSALL

Imogen Hassall was always on the front page of the sixties Sunday papers; bright smile, big tits, sultry-looking, a typical sexy sixties bird — identifiable with Julie Christie, Samantha Eggar and Chelsea. No one really knew much about Imogen's acting career but her image symbolised 'swinging London' with Imogen as one of the first Chelsea birds to live out the sexual revolution, visibly enjoying the freedom and the fun of the new permissive society. Today Imogen Hassall is in her thirties; she still gets publicity, tours Britain in plays, lives in Fulham and is divorced. We talked for two hours, then Imogen drove me home, stopped at a garage and flirted with the attendant almost unconsciously. Sixties pin-up Imogen with her sexy image, and the problems that go with it made me wonder about the seventies pin-up girls with sexy images and how they will cope when they finally hit thirty and look back.

Ten years ago there was no Women's Lib — and a woman was sexually either a servant or a go-getter who went to bed with a man in order to get somewhere. I never slept with men to get any-where — I was just curious and instinctive. It was all a marvellous game and a career and one didn't really care about acting — just this terrific, super time. It was very difficult though — I didn't want the reputation of sleeping around — but on the other hand one was, I suppose, doing it. I had wanted to become a ballet dancer — instead I became a lover.

I spent a good ten years living a very fast life. Chelsea was very 'in' — one was either in Ad-Lib or Annabel's or the White Elephant. I would be in America, in New York, in the nightclubs, where one was known as a jet set girl — and with this jet set girl you slept around. It was a time when men used to phone me in the middle of the night and say, 'Come over'. They weren't treating me with respect, but I used to go. Quite extraordinary. I don't know why I did. I suppose I got a kick out of men ringing me up in the night — others ringing me up in the morning and saying, 'Where the hell were you the night before?' It was something in me that liked to be wanted — it couldn't honestly have been loneliness.

I think at one point I had a reputation going around that I

was a good lover. Of course I wanted to be good — and when a relationship went wrong I used to worry about whether or not I was good in bed. When I was eighteen, nineteen, twenty, twenty-five I used to worry desperately what the other girls were doing and whether I was doing the right thing in bed. They were very well known groovy girls and I thought they must be very abandoned and that they would fuck and screw and then be off.

I had a relationship with someone who is quite well known. He was screwing just about everyone in London — but would always come back to me. I began to be upset that I didn't please him and I wondered where I had gone wrong. I used to think, 'Why doesn't he stay with me?' I realised he must have been getting something else out of the other women. I know now that I used to be too possessive. Men like to get away an awful lot and they thought I wouldn't allow them to.

But I think I knew I was a good lover. I always knew my body was for expression because I was a ballet dancer. I could move my body into different positions — and I knew what a man wanted instinctively. From the age of seven one had learned as a ballet dancer that one's body was beautiful and that one used it. So later you also used it to embrace and entwine a man — like a dancer. I loved the fact that people thought my body was super and photographed me from different angles. I enjoyed people looking at my body and showing it off.

My impact was one of 'there she goes — low cleavage — sexy bird'. I had a head start because men thought I was sexy. You didn't have to do much in bed — you just sort of lay there and the men enjoyed your body. Of course they also expected a great performance from you and I would get upset if I thought I couldn't live up to what someone thought I was.

Men liked me because I was slightly naive and they were getting a feeling of 'she's very young and sweet'. I cheated like mad — I suppose I played a game. Men like to think they are getting something other men haven't had. That they are getting you to do something that you have never done before. So you had to make yourself seem very puritanical and not let men believe you were sleeping around — though you were. I wouldn't get undressed — I wouldn't show my breasts — just because one had flaunted them around. I played a terrific game of bursting into tears and pretending I was a virgin to the end. I did that an awful lot. . .

I was very much like a little girl — terribly childlike and 'whatever you want is good'. I was terribly restricted in bed — until I started feeling sexy. Then I began to be abandoned but it took a long time for the man to get me there. I played a servant role with men — which they adore. I'd cry if they got upset or if I wasn't doing the right thing. Of course asking for what you want in bed is often difficult if you play the servant role — so I would wait until I found the man who gave me what I wanted. Usually though I would be very amicable — I would ask the man to tell me what he wanted — then I would say what I wanted.

Asking for head is very difficult though — I don't think many men want to do it — they don't mind you doing it to them though, for ages. But I always refused what I didn't want in bed. I only forced myself to do something I didn't want sexually in my marriage. It became a nightmare. My husband was physically very handsome — I got married because I thought I ought to — but it was hell — I was on pills — awful.

When I was younger every affair was going to be a new revelation that I was about to live through and learn something from. But I didn't because the men I went out with were very famous. Some of them were awful — it was never you they thought of — it was always I, I, I. They were always much more interested in themselves, in whether they got what they wanted and whether you looked pretty on their arm. Famous men are determined to make you feel they are virile and wonderful and that you are going to walk away and say what a terrific lover they were.

I had one relationship with a major film star who was determined to make me come (I found that frequently with famous men). I couldn't have had an orgasm with a famous man if I had tried — I was so busy thinking of what I ought to be doing. They didn't realise I hadn't come because they thought *they* were marvellous lovers. I started having sex when I was eighteen and I first had an orgasm when I was thirty. Twelve years of complete frustration — but I was a wonderful faker... Sometimes you got a man who went on and on for about six hours. By that time you were exhausted, you wanted breakfast, you couldn't have cared whether you had come — or whether you never saw the man again. And so I faked — and there's even a sort of satisfaction in faking — it's a job like acting.

At last I can admit to myself that I am not acting, I don't

have to pretend any more because after fifteen years of doing what I thought I ought to do, I think I've actually learned to enjoy sex myself — which I didn't before. I have changed enormously sexually — you do get there in the end. After my marriage started to go wrong I began to relax and think — 'so what, I am what I am'. I think I enjoy making love now and I think that makes a good lover. You aren't playing a game, you aren't worried about orgasms — it doesn't matter.

Nowadays I don't go to bed for a long time. I think you should be friends before you become lovers. Unless you see somebody and find them very sexy immediately — which I never do. When I do go to bed with someone I just give everything emotionally and physically. But it's sometimes difficult to avoid going to bed. I don't think I have ever really insulted a man — I usually pretend that he hasn't made a pass at me. But recently I worked with a man for fifteen weeks who'd heard stories about me. He thought I would go to bed with him — but when I didn't he went beserk with sexual aggression and threw me around — I've got a bruise to prove it.

Now I go to bed with younger blokes — they are fascinated by my image, age and experience. You can't really do wrong — they look up to you with such admiration. They give me a lot because now *they* are bright-eyed whereas before *I* was. I used to be all older men and 'show me. . .' but now I am going right the other way. I don't want to whizz off to America any more. I don't want to go to the South of France on an expensive yacht. And I never look at anyone handsome — just people I feel super with. Now *I* want to enjoy my body in bed — that has taken me a long time. I realise I used to play a ridiculous game, because even though I was happy, I also cried a lot.

GERMAINE GREER

'What makes a woman G.I.B?' I don't understand what 'good in bed' means, and I don't know that I have heard men use the phrase. I find the phrase offensive, and I also find offensive the assumption that sex is something that occurs in bed, and not other places. Trying to be a hip fuck is all Dutch to me.

One of the things wrong with the 'jockcratic' society is the assumption that sex is a form of athletics. Sex in the seventies has a Puritanism about it. Everybody has intravaginal intercourse.

In some studies that have been done in the past, it has emerged that Black men and Chicano men give head much more often than white men, and your WASP has got a kind of reversed puritanism. On the one hand he condemns polymorphous sexual activity for other groups like gay people, and when it comes to his sexuality, he is more boring (in both senses of the word) than he has ever been before, because now he doesn't have to practice any of the relative perversions to avoid pregnancy, because the woman is medicated to the eyeballs. He just has intravaginal intercourse. Anal intercourse and coitus interruptus and cunnilingus and fellatio are in abeyance, and you won't find much fellatio in Missouri.

I have always assumed that what really seduced people is the degree of communication that they establish. That's all – and also what makes a woman good in bed is the same as what makes a man good.

The Music World

EARTHA KITT

I saw Eartha Kitt appear at the Stardust Hotel, Las Vegas — a love-sick male fan in his forties was sitting in the front row and Eartha sang 'All By Myself' to him exclusively. The theatre was charged with emotion and after the song the man ran off in tears. The next day, on a local TV show, Eartha described how she had attended a White House Meeting arranged by Lyndon Johnson in order to discuss the problem of black teenagers in America. Johnson appeared briefly for the benefit of TV cameras, the problem was never properly discussed, Eartha complained and it was later revealed that Johnson blacklisted her instantly. So this Las Vegas show was Eartha's first appearance in America since then, although she has been living in Los Angeles with her teenage daughter. When I talked to Eartha she was very passionate about her sexual beliefs, said she wanted the young people to know how she felt, then packed her stage feather boa and drove the six hours back to Los Angeles on her own.

I can make fun of the sex business on stage because I know very well that I am playing a game — I am saying, 'Look at my wares — look — but it doesn't mean that you can have them.' Some men come into my life because they think I will be great in bed — but I immediately detect that and it turns me off. I know men think in terms of conquering me — and I know that many men have bragged that they have been to bed with me when they haven't. I have even heard stories that I have been to bed with two or three men at the same time — I am much too shy to go that route. And the idea just makes me feel unclean all over.

I am a very old-fashioned girl. To me, there's a tremendous honour about having sex with a man. I think it is a pity women are using sex to get a man — that makes every woman into a whore. I don't think in terms of going to bed with a man in order to conquer him. Nor do I think in terms of getting a man because I want to be taken care of — women are often brought up to try and find a man for the wrong reasons — for paying their bills. I don't think in those terms since I am perfectly capable of paying my own bills.

I think sex is more important from a man's point of view than from a woman's. I only go to bed with a man whom I feel is going

71

to be around me for more than just the sexual act. I don't think I have ever been to bed with a man I didn't really care for. The *man's* intentions might have been different from mine — but my feeling is always, 'If I go to bed with you — I want you to be around for a long time.' I look for a man I feel I can live with for the rest of my life in a very romantic way. I don't think you should bother to have a relationship with a man unless you have the feeling you might want to have a child by him. That anyway, is how *I* feel about my own sexual relationships — which I think are very honourable. I look for an honourable man whose intentions are clean and proper — because I have clean and proper intentions myself.

Men today seem able to go to bed with any woman they fancy. They seem to be hunting in a derogatory way — hunting to throw a woman into bed rather than hunting for a relationship. But I also think women have become as much the hunters as men were. Nowadays women lie down *first* and *then* say, 'Have me' which is wrong. If the woman is too willing she will never keep the man. I would rather wait before going to bed with a man — I don't want any man — or anybody — myself in particular — to think of me as a quickie.

I have had incidents where men want to buy me a drink. They thought they were going to get me high because of the drink and then throw me into bed. But if a man pushes me in any way he turns me off. I am so particular about whom I go to bed with that it is very difficult nowadays to find a man who wants to take the time. I like a man who takes his time — takes the time to woo a woman — whether it takes an hour, seven days or a whole year. I like a man who builds up a romantic feeling because those are the memories a woman will live on and want to enhance — the building up to the act. Not the act. The by-play rather than the play itself is much more important to me than seeing somebody that I want to have a sexual relationship with and immediately going to bed with him.

So I tell a man, 'I don't want to go to bed yet — don't rush me.' If a man can't take it — can't wait — then he's not worth having. Because if he really wants you — he will take his time. Then when you get to the sex relationship it will be really appreciated and will be much more enjoyable. And the man will know you are not cheap. I think the old-fashioned way is really the best. A man *says*

he wants a whore in bed. But what he really wants is a *lady* whore
— a woman he can also respect — not a woman who is just there to
have sex with. And I want a man to respect me.

It is very difficult to say how a woman should behave before
bed or in bed. Because you behave according to how the man
behaves. The man has got to be half of the game. If I feel that the
man is rough in any way, verbally or physically — I get turned off.
I know how I feel about myself and I don't want any man to
abuse me.

I think a man makes a woman good in bed. And so does the
relationship between them — the way they feel about each other —
that soft gentility — that wonderful feeling that nature has
brought you together. During the sex act a woman should relax
— she shouldn't stiffen. But that only happens if the woman
doesn't have a strong feeling for the man. If you are really
emotionally involved with a man, admire him, and have tremendous respect for him, you can just relax and let nature take its
course. So much depends on the man and your feelings for him.

In my case younger men are usually much better partners. They
want me because they recognise my sensuality. I have always
preferred men who wanted me for my sensuality rather than for
sex. And also younger men often have had tremendous respect
for their mothers and see signs of their mother in me.

In my maturing years I have suddenly realised that I don't
feel I need sex as much today as I thought I needed it when I
was much younger. Therefore, I have also become even more
choosy about men than when I was younger. It takes me a long
time to find a man I really want to have a sexual relationship
with. Which is probably why I don't have a man in my life at
the moment.

TONY BENNETT

'What makes a woman G.I.B?' Coming together.

ISAAC HAYES

Isaac Hayes sat by his Bel Air pool, in long, white woolly
pants, which were inexplicably baggy all over. A lady who

may, or may not, have been his wife wandered in and out of the house, until the interview began. Then I sat on a sofa — very close to Isaac Hayes and the lady sat opposite. At the end of the interview he got up and began to strum on the piano and sing, 'What the World needs now is love'. Isaac also told me that he would like to make a really sexy record —the tape of this interview would be perfect.

The ideal woman for me would be a superwoman in bed — a woman who is very, very long-winded and can make love for hours, especially when my appetite is sharp. She must be able to please me with foreplay to the point of almost uncontrollable desire. She must be creative, with a lot of imagination, so she is capable of being different things — for example, more or less like a slave sometimes. A woman who is very uninhibited, who would say, do, or feel anything that she wanted to during sex, including oral sex — the whole trip. A woman with endurance, with a lot of fire, with warmth, uninhibited, and of course, a good-looking body — that helps.

There are some women who are physically perfect — not body-wise, but in their genital area: the texture and the location of the vaginal canal. Not necessarily tightness; it can be the fatty tissues in the walls of the vagina that add a lot. Also the erotic juices and the secretion of those juices and the overall feel. Sometimes a woman doesn't have to move at all, and can produce an orgasm from a man just effortlessly, whereas others have to work and do all kinds of things, yet still do not get the same results out of a man as the ones with that natural feel.

Vibrations and a sixth sense can detect if a woman is good in bed. I guess you could say my sensuous antennae might be out-stretched, and it could pick up some radiations from a woman. I've been deceived sometimes by women, though; some I would expect great things of and was disappointed, yet with others I wasn't expecting great things, but was pleasantly surprised.

I find the more common-looking or unattractive women are much better in bed than the very, very attractive women. It seems as if beautiful women are too hung up on their outward appear-ance. Whereas the woman who is not so attractive and knows that all she has is herself and her body is not inhibited by, 'I wonder if I will get my makeup running down my face, or my hair will get messed up.' The unattractive woman doesn't care about that and just gets totally involved and expresses herself. But if you do find a woman who is attractive *and* good in bed, she is dynamite.

I always select the woman who is stand-offish — who seems to be shy, not trying to catch my eye, with avoiding glances. Because you find that the women that are all upfront, wow, waving flags and stuff are very shallow and are trying to do a sales job on you — and I bypass those. Whereas the woman that seems to be shy, not too extraverted, will attract me. Somehow or other I will get to her, get her attention.

Then there are women that seem to be very confident. If I am in the mood for a challenging situation, I like the woman who is very confident and looks as if she is saying, 'I am just as important to me as you are.' If she values herself, then she must *be* of some value. Evidently people have reacted to her that way. There had to have been some experiences to justify her attitude of confidence, so then I want that one, too.

A lot of guys expect too much. They expect a woman to be ready-made and responsive. I think women adjust to a man — so you have to get them prepared for your way of lovemaking; that is why there are some inexperienced women who I enjoy more than an experienced woman, because an inexperienced woman can personally adapt herself to me, to my way of lovemaking. Then she discovers new things and her response is so sincere and so honest. The inexperienced woman is so open — she can bend either way, like a young sapling. If, again, the man is sharp and adept, he can mould her in a way that will please him. But, of course, the experienced woman also has her way of doing things and of pleasing the man.

It's up to the man to put a woman in such a mental state that he will have complete control of her physical faculties. Then he can get what he wants out of her. It doesn't matter to me how long it takes a woman to come, because after a while you know if she is frequently orgasmic or if she is infrequently orgasmic. Then you can just build according to the way she wants you to. You can tell by her body language, by her reaction in bed. Then, after several sexual involvements with her, you should really know where to take her.

Some women are multiple-orgasmic; I have known women (I have counted for my own satisfaction) within a ten-hour period to average about fifty orgasms. Then there are those who can only stand one – they are so sensitive that you have to wait so many minutes. The orgasms that take a long time to reach are much stronger than the ones reached quickly, because so much tension and build-up has occurred, so when the woman comes, it just explodes; it's violently strong.

There are some women who are almost totally frigid, with so many mental hang-ups due to the formative years of their maturing, and almost nothing can be done about it. The woman who is bad in bed is very dry, has no juices, very little secretions. She doesn't move, doesn't respond, and is too bashful or ashamed to respond to you.

In the past a woman was supposed to be a lady at all times, even in bed – which is a taboo that cursed a lot of marriages, causing men to drift and look for pleasure elsewhere. And so a lot of guys turn to hookers, because they are uninhibited. Whereas the wife – after it's done – jumps up and washes, and never utters another word until the next day at the breakfast table.

I feel that a woman should be free to say, feel, and do whatever she wants. A sexual experience should be total and completely free. Sometimes a woman will not do something because she is afraid of what the man will think of her. So I think that the man should really tell the woman up front, 'Hey, whatever you want to do, you tell me – you tell me what you want me to do, whatever you do is all right.'

Women should ask for what they want and not expect a man to be a know-it-all. Sex should be a mutual thing of communication where both partners can exchange different ideas and different feelings and thoughts. Both involved should strive for mutual satisfaction, so there should also be mutual investment of exchange of knowledge and of interest.

I have found that if a woman refuses something in bed, she can be a challenge. Then I make suggestions sometimes and the woman says, 'No, I don't want to do that.' So I say, 'You don't know what you are missing.' And she says, 'Well, I will never know.' But then we keep working on it and I take another approach – sneak up on her blind side, so before she realizes it, she is enjoying what she said she wouldn't do. After a while she really gets to like it and even becomes very aggressive with it. So later on, when you talk about it, she says, 'Wow, just think what I have been missing.'

I feel that with a woman I can cover three hundred and sixty degrees of activities from one extreme to another — from a sadistic to a masochistic attitude. Some women like you to be very warm and tender — which I can be — a woman like that can arouse me by being very warm and tender. Other women like you to be very, very sadistic and violent with them in bed — which I can be also.

Chatter in bed really turns me on. The more a woman talks and really lets me know how she feels, it arouses me, because to utter vulgarities is sometimes a turn-on! Also, another thing which turns me on are the natural body odours which generate between two people. They are quite stimulating — not unhygienic, but the ones that arise out of the actual excitement and the activity.

I have experienced sex with women all over the world and I find that Latin women are very torrid, uninhibited lovers. There are good lovers of all races, but I guess I lean towards the exotic: the Oriental, Filipino, Hawaiian, Mexican, and of course the Black woman.

Basically, the Black woman is what I have known all my life, and for me she is best in bed. I find that in the past decade Black women have become more free with their sexual activities. One thing that I really appreciate about the Black woman is her physical make-up, especially in her genital area, where it's very strong — with the durability to withstand and endure sex. A lot of women of other nationalities are weak, and after a very healthy session they pain or sometimes might even spot. But a Black woman is very strong, and I guess you can look at it hereditarily: working in the fields, having a baby, and then getting up the next day and going back to work.

ENGELBERT HUMPERDINCK

'What makes a woman G.I.B?' It isn't physical. It's in the eyes of the beholder — in the eyes of the woman. But what makes a woman good in bed also stems from the well known American saying, 'God grant me the serenity to accept the things I can't change, courage to change the things I can — and the wisdom to know the difference.

ROGER DALTREY

Who lead singer, Roger Daltrey has got beautiful blue eyes, an intelligent ex-model wife, Heather, and two children, Rosie Lee and Willow — both, which Roger says, were 'the result of two really great fucks. I think really great fucks produce lovely children — I really feel that.' Roger Daltry lives in an Elizabethan Manor in Sussex — which should be incongruous but somehow isn't. With his long blonde curls Roger looks decidedly nineteenth century — straight out of 'Lisztomania', his last film. Roger was shy at the beginning of the interview then became very nostalgic and vocal about groupies not being the way they used to be. Heather was very interested in the G.I.B. book. She and Roger wanted to know what technique hints I had learned and presented me with a pair of edible 'candy pants' before I left.

Around 1968 there was a clique of groupies that were the best ever. They were really great in bed — incredible, fantastic fucks. They were proud of being groupies — totally servile — groupies *have* to be servile. Groups on the road are absolute pigs — they have to be in order to survive — it's such an unnatural life — town to town — room to room. You get very little time on the road to romance anybody, so groupies make life easier. There is no way you can say, 'I'd like to get to know you.' It's just, 'Stay here and fuck — or else fuck off.'

Groupies don't actually suggest going to bed with you — you just say, 'Get your gear off' and they get their gear off. Or else you get into bed — there's three women there and it just happens. They just want to fuck you to score you up. Groupies don't have special techniques in bed — they are just very easy to get there. . . But a few of them do know some tricks; baby oil and a cold flannel — they rub the baby oil all over your prick — put a cold flannel on your balls — and then give you head. Very nice. Or whipped cream over the whole body —then fucking — it's really great. Only trouble is — it dries up and goes a bit sticky — but when you first do it — it's really fantastic.

I still see a lot of the old groupies as friends. Before — when our group was often in one place and we had more time, the old groupies made sure they built up a relationship with you apart from the fucking. They used to cook for you — travel with you —

everything. They still wanted to score you up, but they also wanted to fuck you in order to give you a good time – and they also had a good time themselves because they really had a thing about making love. But it all changed suddenly when groupies started getting a lot of publicity.

I fucked around a lot on the road before I was married and I'm not ashamed of pulling groupies, but it's a long time since I had one. I don't think the last ones I had were that good. You felt as if you were just another notch on whatever they put their notches on – that they were just fucking you to say they had done it. To say, 'I fucked him – and I fucked him' – so what?

I found a lot of the new groupies' minds were somewhere else when they were screwing you – probably living out their fantasies – not really getting into you, just fucking your photograph. You got a feeling that they were doing their act rather than enjoying it. That doesn't turn me on when I am with a woman. Groupies do a lot of things just because they're expected of them.

Groupies usually come in twos, then if you get a good duet – they are really great. The same two usually work together and sometimes they work on each other. I think women are much more likely to be bisexual than guys are. I've never been with a guy – but there are a lot of women that go with other women – not lesbians – just women who really get off on cuddling each other. Women really do like to be cuddled and made a fuss of. I don't think a lot of guys do that – they just stick their cock up a woman. So I think some women miss the cuddling which is why they go with other women.

Really I think women get better in bed as they get older. But then – I've had a lot of really young chicks that have been great. It sounds terribly *blasé* but I've had a lot of virgins in my time and most of them have been incredible – instantly good in bed. I think a woman can be taught to be good and maybe those virgins were good because they hadn't been with anybody else so they got used to everything I did. Anyway I've never had a bad virgin – they have all been naturally good.

I think a woman is born good in bed – but women who are bad are bad because they have had too much fucking and not enough loving. You meet chicks who've had one or two blokes but have no idea and just lay there like a dead dog. Some women don't open up at all – but when you first meet them you think they will be really good. You are in a room with fifty people – a girl keeps staring at you – rubs against you – and slips you her phone number. But once you get her into bed – she's quite a let down. The sort of woman who is quite shy and reserved is usually far better in bed than raucous, loud, obvious chicks who usually open up far less.

If a woman doesn't come it just screws your head up. It makes me feel inadequate if I try everything I know and the woman still doesn't come. It does kind of turn me off. You can still enjoy fucking the woman but if she doesn't come, it does make you feel that you are not good enough for her. At least, that's how it makes *me* feel. The trouble is – a guy comes every time – whereas a woman can literally fuck fifty men till she finds one man that she can come with. Of course women fake. Sure – I can tell if a woman is faking. No doubt about it – they just don't move right. You can feel it, especially if you're a musician like I am and into rhythm.

I am a very active fuck – a speed freak – very energetic and if I make love with a woman who wants to do it on top – or to do lots of fast moving – we are both moving so fast that we never make contact. And I find if a woman fucks like I do we are incompatible – because we are too similar. I can fuck very few women who fuck like I do. I really feel that the man should dominate in bed and I hate a woman trying to fuck me.

I find it is more difficult for me to be really at ease with beautiful chicks I don't know. Beforehand, beautiful women can obviously get you very mentally worked up, but it's really difficult to open up to a really beautiful chick – especially on a one night stand. I am not sure if beautiful women are better in bed – but tall women really turn me on. When you are nose to nose, your toes are in it – when you are toes to toes, your nose is in it and when *you* are in it you don't know whether you are coming or going.

Sometimes, with my wife, we feel like being cuddly and really laid back – but other times you want to go on like a couple of raving nymphomaniacs. Sex really depends on the mood you're in at the time. Before, there were some nights when I really fancied someone who was intelligent, who I could talk to – a chick you really wanted to make love to because you really wanted to know her that much better. To me there are two different types of fucking — the other kind is when you fancy a really whorey, tarty chick — total lust. Then with those chicks it's almost like a fanny wank.

Most women think masturbation is bad — which is ridiculous. Half the women I've met don't masturbate, but I think all women who are really open about sex do. I've met an awful lot of women who use vibrators so much that they can't come any other way — I am sure it damages the nerve ends.

I think more guys masturbate than women do — and masturbation takes a lot out of them. So when they do make love to a woman — they want that bit extra, otherwise they can just have a wank. They want closeness. Just for the time you are making love to a woman you want to feel as if you are one. I think guys kind of need that. At least *I* feel that way.

The best chicks I've ever had in bed really gave themselves 100 percent. You are so close that even if the phone rings — it fucking rings and you don't even hear it — that's pretty rare though. A woman is really great when you make love to her and feel that you are *both* making love 100 percent and nothing else. That makes a chick great. Even a great groupie show doesn't equal that. Sometimes you got three of four groupies in bed at one time. It seemed to fit in with the madness of being on the road; it's such a mad, ridiculous way of life that four women in bed seemed natural. It's fun — it's good for a laugh. But I find that you get over-excited having three or four women at once — parts of bodies everywhere — everything going on. I think it gets boring in the end — it's just the lust part of sex. You don't get 100 percent into it — a lot of things are happening — then it's over — and that's it. It was never as good as being with the one chick you are really fond of, who gives herself 100 percent to you.

SONNY BONO

'What makes a woman G.I.B?' Good bloodline, background and breeding.

BARRY WHITE

I met rock star Barry White by accident. I was living in Hollywood in a Sunset Boulevard block of flats known as

81

'the beginning and the end' — people either begin there with no money or end there with no money. One day, an excited friend told me she was convinced that Barry White had just gone into the next flat. I didn't believe her — I knew what *I* was doing at 'the beginning and the end' — but Barry White's presence there was surprising. Nevertheless — I still rang the door bell — a man appeared wearing a white woollen cap and a gold ring with the initials B.W. I asked him if he was Barry White — he said yes — he was Barry White and yes — he would do an on-the-spot interview. So we did — although until 'Barry' signed a release I wasn't convinced that I was talking to *the* Barry White. I knew that initial caution about his identity was advisable, remembering a Las Vegas launderette where the owner proudly showed me a shirt she said belonged to Ringo Starr. Apparently he had given her his autograph, washed his shirt himself, then left it to dry, and was about to collect it. Eventually, 'Ringo' appeared, with a 13-year-old girlfriend, glass rings on his fingers, holes in his shoes — and a Texas accent.

My woman has to be a perfect woman because I'm a perfectionist. I'm a Virgo. The way that I choose a woman is by her star sign. She has to be one of my signs because I know which signs I like and can relate to. I can get along with any women, but it's whether or not I want to go through the trip with them. I deal in horoscopes and personalities, and I've had every woman in the horoscope — two of each — and their personalities are identifiable by their star signs.

To me, some of the greatest women are Leo women, Gemini women, Libra women, Taurus women, and Capricorn women — it's in their makeup. A true Capricorn woman is feminine; she knows she's feminine, she likes being feminine, and that's what makes her so good. She also can adapt to anything her man wants. Libra woman can stay at one balance — they don't change much, which a man likes. Taurus women can flex with a man; they know how to flex. A Taurus woman can take a weak man and make him think he is strong; because of the way she deals with men, she upgrades a man instead of trying to downgrade him until the upgrading becomes outrageous.

The worst thing a woman can do in bed is to be something that she is not – especially with me, because I can tell. Women always overact. I like sex to flow naturally. I am in command because I am a man, so it is important for me to understand, creatively, what I am doing to a woman in bed. I want to know how to do it, to that *particular* woman. There are a lot of men who don't care what they do to a woman, as long as they are satisfied.

It doesn't matter if a woman takes a long time to come. That depends on the man, how much the woman is into him and what he knows. A woman isn't less good if she asks for what she wants in bed; it depends on *how* she asks, and *what* she asks. A woman should always be honest just like a man should, and say what it is, say what she means, and mean what she says. It's in my nature to analyse a conversation with anybody, not just a woman. You meet women who say things like, 'I'm not interested in money.' That could be true, yet it may not be true. There are times when it isn't so. I like to find out the truth.

Women are very gullible. They see Barry White and they fall apart. They should never do that, because I'm a human being like the rest of the men. The only difference is that I have a job which keeps me in front of a lot of other women. Women always want something that another woman wants. They can't help that, but they should try to control it and be honest.

There isn't any special age group of woman who are good in bed. I've seen women of nineteen be equally good as women of forty-five. But there's no doubt about it, love makes a woman good in bed. I know so. The women that don't have it are very miserable, and the ones that do are very happy.

I don't get hung up on the things that other men get hung up on. They get hung up on a woman's looks and what she has got on, then want to go to bed with her. Men meet a woman and think she is so beautiful that no matter what is wrong with her personality, 'I'll go along with it.' Well, I am not that way. Shit, no! I don't give a fuck how a woman looks – if she ain't together, it's over, there's nothing to talk about. I can usually tell by talking to a woman, by having a conversation with her, what she is basically looking for, sexually, because me, when I am talking to a woman, I just talk to her, I am listening to what she is saying, analysing what she is saying. Then I can tell what she wants in life, how she looks at life, how she faces problems every day.

Refusing what she doesn't want in bed is the prerogative of a woman. After all, she is an individual. A lot of men try to take that from women — being an individual. Me, I like to enhance it. If I find a woman who has a beautiful personality and is a beautiful person, I don't subtract from it and I don't add to it. In any case, everybody's opinion of what makes a woman good in bed has to be different, because everybody doesn't see the same person in the same way.

DEBBIE REYNOLDS

'What makes a woman G.I.B?' I am not exactly the sexy one to ask, I suppose. I think first of all to go to bed to sleep, you should exercise a great deal. To go to bed to be a great love mate, you have to love the man a great deal.

BIANCA JAGGER

I phoned Bianca Jagger one evening when she was in London for the Stones' Knebworth concert. A lady answered the phone and said she was the maid. I had an instinct that she wasn't — so I still told her about my book. And when I finished the 'maid' said, 'This is Bianca Jagger — I would like to read your manuscript.' So I finally took it round to the Jaggers' house in Chelsea late that night. Bianca opened the door herself — in a white cotton nightie, wearing no make-up. We sat on the floor on large cushions, Bianca ordered Chinese food from Mr. Chow's Restaurant — and we talked about love, sex, men and relationships until dawn. She agreed to be interviewed; while we were talking Mick phoned and Bianca told me she would love to know what *he* thought made a woman good. She was very curious about the G.I.B. book, wanted to know which celebrities I liked best, which celebrities I had fancied, which had made a pass at me and what I had learned while writing the book. Bianca looked very small, very thin, very childlike, smiled a great deal and kept running her fingers through her hair. Altogether unlike her public image; not at all haughty, never once name-dropped — was far more interested in discussing relationships than fashion and beauty — and I was struck by her perceptive intelligence.

84

I need to be flirtatious; I am what the French call *une allumeuse*; I like to light every fire possible. Because I feel I behave in a very manly way, even being very feminine physically and in my behaviour, my mind is manly, so sometimes I feel insecure and I need to feel that maybe men find me attractive. I'm always scared that when people meet me they will either think that I am frigid or that I am not capable of doing anything. But in fact I am very romantic, not conservative, but shy. I feel that I have not experienced — I don't believe in all the tricks — I am completely vulnerable, as if I were thirteen. In a way, I suppose, each time a woman goes to bed with a man she is a little bit of a virgin.

I was brought up in a very feudal society; my parents were very puritanical, so I was brought up to believe that you remain a virgin until you marry a man. You could not be presented to marry someone if you were not a virgin. You asked me if I was ever scared to refuse something in bed. Well, I was brought up to believe that so many things should be refused, even within marriage. When I was a little girl we had lessons at school and I heard about all the things that were 'accepted within wedlock' and all the things that were not. Natural things were accepted — and unnatural things were not. And I always wondered what the hell natural things were — and for years after I still believed some things were 'natural'.

Thirteen years of convent life do not go away in one minute; no matter what you do, they are still there. I think I have a lot of guilt about sex deep, deep inside my subconscious, even if my intelligence refuses to accept it. But then some studies of women show that guilt is very, very important for sexual satisfaction — that a woman who has no guilt whatsoever just does it like having lunch or playing tennis. I sometimes admire a woman who is capable of having sexual relations with a man just because she wants him sexually. But I am incapable of doing that; I can't just go and meet somebody and say, 'Well, why not?'

When I was still a virgin I went to live in France. I felt so vulnerable, such a little girl, so inexperienced and naive. Being a virgin was so peculiar at that time in Paris. I was so scared — I thought, 'What would a man do?' I always used to feel inferior to the other girls because I was a virgin and they had affairs and were free. Then one day I realized that being free is not doing everything that is available to you, but eliminating all the things you don't want to do and waiting for the one you do want. People who are free don't need to prove anything. They don't need to prove they can fuck every man. Freedom is to be able to say to a man, 'I don't want to fuck you because I either want to be on my own, or I love somebody to whom I want to be faithful.'

But a lot of men try to make you feel insecure if you refuse them. They say, 'Are you frigid?' or that maybe you don't feel anything, maybe you are not sensual, maybe you are not sexual. They think if they accuse you of being frigid you will go to bed with them. That happened a lot when I was an adolescent in Paris. And maybe because I first started to be a woman in France – always, even today, I feel like a little girl when I am there – and Frenchman always make me feel insecure. Every time a Frenchman asks me to have a cup of coffee I still feel like a virgin, as if I can't cope and wouldn't know what to do if he made a pass at me.

An Englishman can invite you to have a cup of tea in his house – he will offer you a cup of tea – then, if it happens, it happens. But a Frenchman will invite you to his house and tell you to come and have breakfast with croissants. Not only will he expect you to go to bed with him, but he will probably expect you to make breakfast as well. And if you refuse to go to bed with him, he will find a reason to hurt you – will become intent on making you feel you're not a woman of the world, and are unsophisticated or frigid.

Nowadays I say, 'Am I supposed to be frigid because I don't want to fuck you?' Or I say, 'I couldn't,' or, 'I feel so tired.' or, 'Mick...' Being married is a marvellous asset, you know, and people accept it very willingly. Except sometimes they say, 'Oh, well, I thought you were more *en vogue* and free. You are really so bourgeois.' But it's not important what other people think, it's what you know about yourself.

I was in love for a long, long time with a man who was much older than me. He made me feel secure, had tolerance. I wanted protection, I wanted affection, I wanted tenderness and someone who was not the kind of person who didn't care what I felt, what I wanted, or who just wanted to take me. I was always afraid of making love to a man who made me feel as if I was being taken, of a man who did not share anything with me, but was making love to a reflection of himself, as if one was an object that reflected his own image – but had no contact with him. Not an exchange, but being with someone who looks at you as if you were transparent.

I hate the idea of being taken unless I decide that I want to be taken, and I only decide that when I know that the man is willing to give himself and when there's no longer a relationship of power. I am fascinated by power – but I am terrified if somebody else exerts it over me. Power is the great game between men and women which men think they have won – but that is not true because the greatest power over a politician, creative artist and intellectual has always been the secret power women have. Someone once said that the power women have over men is when they discover a man's weakness and then reassure him.

A woman's secret power is not just being good in bed. Everybody is a potential great lover – unless they are physically insensitive. Every man can make a woman into a great lover, and every woman can make a man into a great lover. But I don't believe being good in bed has anything to do with techniques. It's to do with love, with emotions, tenderness, and intellect. It is also to do with the freedom a man makes you feel, the tenderness you see in him, and the confidence he gives you because confidence makes you daring. You dare to do things with someone who makes you feel confident about yourself, about your behaviour, about your morals. A woman is sometimes afraid to be sexually free because she thinks, 'If I was really myself and really show what I want sexually and sensually, maybe he will underestimate me and think I am some kind of a tart.'

You shouldn't have to ask for what you want in bed. I hate words. I think that if you have any amount of communication and understanding, you don't need to use words unless the man is selfish and assumes there are things that are due to him and not to the woman. I would advise a woman to be with a man who gives her tenderness. And an intellectual woman should be with a man she has respect for, to be sexually turned on by someone I need, to a certain extent, to have respect and esteem for him. Otherwise, sexually, he wouldn't interest me whatsoever. If I don't respect the person, he becomes nonexistent to me.

I think the obsession with orgasm is a great problem in our society. A great deal of sexual dissatisfaction is due to the fact that people think the orgasm is so essential. If you study old civilizations like the Incas and the Egyptians, you find that the period before the orgasm is what is important. I don't believe in faking; being truthful matters in bed, and I don't fake. I think one shouldn't only when you try to avoid pain for somebody you love

When you love somebody you want to give them as much pleasure as you can. People talk about marvellous Japanese girls who know every sexual secret and then one feels so limited. When you really love somebody you feel so jealous of somebody else who is able to give them more pleasure than you did. I would never really dare ask a man if I was good in bed. But when I meet a man who is successful (I am very fascinated by people that have success — I sometimes feel I should be ashamed of liking success and people who have it) you feel so insecure because there you stand and you think they must have known some extraordinary woman that were so beautiful, so intelligent, maybe so marvellous in bed. And that is why I always want to say, 'Who is the woman, what did she do that maybe I could do, how was she that maybe I could be better?'

So I ask them, 'Who was the woman that you thought was sexually the greatest?' And then they pretend and say, 'Of course you,' and then I said, 'I wasn't asking about me.' Anyway, you feel they're lying because you always think there was somebody more extraordinary physically, that there was somebody more sensually free, more experienced. You always think that even when you believe they really desire you, when you believe they really love you, when you feel they're really touched by you and really moved by you, that maybe in their mind there is still a myth — somebody else they loved and desired that you will never ever be able to surpass.

I have felt incredibly, incredibly inconfident — you can walk into a room, feel you're fantastic and everybody looks at you, but you know that still doesn't mean anything when you're really close to a man. Because he can feel, 'She is so beautiful, but anyway I don't want her.' Or he can want a beautiful woman to own like you own beautiful objects or you own beautiful paintings. Being beautiful, being glamorous and looking wonderful does not mean that a man will want you. Being beautiful and being good in bed alone won't satisfy a person.

I have talked about emotions and tenderness, but it is passion that is extraordinary. Passion is part of your character — some women are born passionate. Passion is being able to make love to a person and go beyond life and into death. For me fantasy is so much more important than reality. My dream — I am so romantic that for me the greatest thing will always be a book by Saint Exupery called *The Little Prince*. I shouldn't say it (because he is so arrogant) but when I met Mick he became for me the Little Prince and the rest was part of reality, but with him it was all part of fantasy. When you get that with somebody who could talk fantasy, then the rest doesn't matter.

Until Mick the search was for a father figure — for the protection and affection a father can provide. And the day I think I grew up a little bit — the day I didn't need a father figure any more — was when I fell in love with Mick because he was my older brother — he was no longer the father.

Mick taught me that being vulnerable and needing somebody and loving somebody and being able to say that is not weak. Before Mick I was incapable of that. I never thought somebody could want, need, and be dependent on somebody without losing their dignity. Mick taught me that because he is capable of doing it without ever losing his dignity. People think that if they are capable of being vulnerable they will lose their dignity. One almost never dares say things like, 'I need you, I love you.' A real relationship is when one is capable of saying that, while always keeping your dignity and nevertheless with the understanding that if the person didn't want you, you wouldn't want them any more — because you like yourself.

I do feel threatened by other women wanting Mick, but you could feel threatened with any man, because they are all human. No matter who he is, he may turn a corner tomorrow and find a woman he thinks much more extraordinry than the one he has at home. But that's the risk everybody in the world has, every man and every woman. But if things are going to be ended, they are going to be ended anyway. The intelligent thing is not to think about how insecure you should be, but try to be balanced within the situation. You have to have something with somebody beyond sex and physique and success, something very, very special that goes beyond all the superficial and trivial things, that gives you the feeling that you have something with somebody that nobody else has, something timeless. Being good in bed is not timeless.

GLADYS KNIGHT

'What makes a woman G.I.B?' Seriously, it's up to the individual — you may be good to someone but you may not be good to someone else.

ANGIE BOWIE

Angie Bowie, at 27, is a year older than me — yet treats me like a daughter. We had met before when I interviewed Angie for a 1974 radio programme. I remember her then; very thin, very intense, very hypertense, eyes glowing: 'All I ever wanted was to be in the movies — to *be* the movies.' When I met Angie this time in London she was actually on her way to audition for 'the movies'. I never discovered *which* particular movie — but I *did* know that Angie's plan to star in a film of Ruth Ellis' life has not yet materialised. David Bowie was hardly mentioned but I remembered stories of the Bowie's transatlantic marriage, their little son Zowie already going to Beverly Hills parties and Angie's rumoured competitiveness with David's career. She has posed for countless fashion spreads, gives magazine interviews and appeared on the Russell Harty show looking stunning. Angie Bowie gives the impression that she is going somewhere quite special — but as yet unspecified — in terms of her own career. She talked to me about her sexuality over lunch at a Chelsea restaurant, in an accent which is a curious mixture of Beverly Hills and Beckenham.

Over the years, bisexuality has become identifiable with me because David and I admitted we were bisexual — there are a bunch of young chicks who realised their own bisexuality and sort of held one up as a pin-up. David and I used to have a lot of scenes with other girls. We were twenty minutes late for our own wedding though because we were having a scene with another girl. We had got up early that morning and decided to have another chick; she was a beautiful girl — an actress. So we were late for the wedding.

Men never made me feel I wasn't good in bed — but some chicks did. I first went to bed with a chick when I was sixteen. I didn't have the faintest idea what to do, so I was totally instinctive. I lived in Cyprus, where women are built like hour glasses; so I hadn't had any interest in my own body, in being tall and thin, having no tits, and really long legs. Until I suddenly realised that this chick I was in bed with was really getting off on all those things. So going to bed with a chick made me realise how 'beautiful' I was.

I don't think there is any difference between being good in bed with a girl and being good in bed with a man. It depends on how you feel that day. Although I have become much more patient — going to bed with chicks because they do take a long time to come. So you have to be very unselfish and very good with them. Just recently I seem to be having this amazing affect on young chicks of about 18 — which really upsets me. I want to protect them but a lot of these young chicks have really been chasing me, making passes. I've never thought of myself like that — I've always had trips with chicks who were my own age — who I was really close to, thought a great deal of, admired.

I first went to bed with a man when I was eighteen. My father wouldn't let me go to bed with anyone when I was younger, so I had promised him to wait until I was eighteen. And I think that all those years of passionate ragings produced hallucinatory manifestations of what you did once you got into bed. So I felt fucking relieved when I finally went to bed with a man. I suppose I liked it — I don't remember too much about it. I think I had probably made sex so monumental in my mind that I was at a loss. I was with the guy for quite a while, so it must have been alright, or I wouldn't have hung around. I didn't always come when I went to bed with men; but that was totally unimportant and never bothered me one way or another. I am too butch—.

I always imagine that I am totally undemanding sexually — but I am sure that is not true — I'm sure I am dreadful. There are a lot of things I won't do unless I'm feeling devilish. I never get into oral sex unless it's with someone serious. I never suck someone's dick until after about eight months — when they've promised me their life and their children. Then I know they are serious — I'm not having any fucking asshole walking around saying I've sucked his dick.

I've never gone to bed with somebody because I didn't have anything better to do. I only go if I'm more interested in that person than in being by myself. And I'm not at all into wanking — I can't be bothered — I'm too much into acting — I like to have an audience. The most people I've had sex in front of was ten — I felt magnificent — I wouldn't have done it if I hadn't known I would feel magnificent. I had a man and a couple of chicks that time at my house in London.

I spend my happiest and best hours with my *rorting* team — rorting means screwing chicks. There's four or five guys and me and all we do is pick up chicks and have a laugh and see who can poke them first. We've been doing this for many years; you have to pick a chick up and she has to agree to be fucked with no-one leaving the room — not in private. She has to understand that from the off — that its like a communal effort — like living theatre. She doesn't have to be fucked by more than the one person she fancies. What she can't do is lay down the conditions of how, when or where. And everybody watches.

The best chicks I've watched or fucked are the ones who have as much nerve as guys. So that they don't have any sexual hang ups and it doesn't upset them to fuck someone while there are other people around. I think the best girls also have a penchant for theatre — for dressing up. So you can say to them, 'Go on — put on that corset, those stockings, those silver boots.' I like to see a really good show. On the other hand, some of the best chicks I've fucked in front of guys were dikes. The guys love it and they always have hysterics, seeing a chick able to get another chick off.

Being good in bed is nothing to do with keeping a man. That is being charming, frivolous, understanding life, having a sense of humour. I kept a man like David by proving that he would never get anyone as magnificent — but it had nothing to do with bed. Although it *is* sexual, in as much as everyone else wanted you so he could always think: 'Well — I'm very fortunate, seeing as how I've got her.' It's that kind of pride.

I reckon if you want to be good in bed — you are — no tricks whatsoever. You can't *not* be good at something if you are going to indulge in it. Being good in bed is for your own charisma, your own pride, your own noblesse. If you admit failure in sex or your career — or any area, you are failing as an individual. If you come to the conclusion that you are not being as good as you could be — then you have to decide whether you are going to accept it (which is immediately an enormous blow to your confidence) or you can totally refuse to accept failure. I always refuse to have anything to do with it. There's nobody I've ever been to bed who when I walk into a restaurant ever ignores me, ever. No-one. I can honestly tell you no matter who I see in a restaurant — no matter what I've done with them — no matter how outrageous — we greet each other with squeals of delight. And if that ever changed, I'd know I'd become less of a person.

SUSAN GEORGE

'What makes a woman G.I.B?' The person she is in bed with.

Media Men and Women

MICHAEL PARKINSON

I was worried about this interview as I expected Michael
Parkinson to steamroller me with Northern finality. I felt
very Southern and plummy as he poured vinegar on his chips
over lunch at Burkes, a fashionable London dining club. I
wasn't just intimidated by the North, but also by Michael's
initial reaction over the phone, 'I won't take the subject
seriously, you know.' However, although I expected to be
'sent up', Michael concentrated on the interview, was quick,
sharp, sometimes flip, but always courteous. And, in spite of
himself, took the subject seriously.

I don't think that the physical act matters – the woman's fifty
orgasms and the guy keeping it up for four hours – I don't think
that matters. I mean – *I* can't keep it up for four hours – for
Christ's sake – and I've never been with a woman who's had fifty
orgasms. The trouble with sex today is that people think you can
measure it in terms of star ratings and how many orgasms each
partner scores.

I have been married for seventeen years to the same woman
and according to the magazines – according to the mystery of the
orgasm and that sort of crap – it's not perfect. Not by those
standards. But it *is* perfect, because we love each other; we allow
for each other's mistakes and we laugh at them.

You have to be able to laugh at your own foolishness. I have
made some bloody awful physical mistakes and I had to laugh at
myself, otherwise it would have been disaster. That's where I
got my sense of humour from – in bed. I don't know how I ever
got it together again after my first sexual experience. I was a
serving officer in the British Army, and I was having it off with
a rather large barmaid in a field in Salisbury. Suddenly a torch was
shone upon me and a man said, 'My name is Sergeant Potter of
the Salisbury Constabulary.' I turned round, the light was in my
eyes, and I was very embarrassed. Eventually, though, my eyes
got accustomed to the glare. And I could see that although the
man had a policeman's helmet on, he wasn't wearing any trousers,
and what's more – he wasn't holding a truncheon in his left hand
– but a winkle... So I pursued Sergeant Potter across this
meadow in Salisbury, but I couldn't catch him and I later discovered that he apparently was a well-known flasher... I don't

97

know how I ever recovered from that traumatic first experience.

Although it is every man's dream that he is going to meet the greatest lover in the world who's going to be tender and loving and lead him to it — there was no *one* woman who suddenly made it happen for me. Projecting back to when I was single, I didn't always have to sense a lasting relationship with a woman but just to feel that I might conceivably grow to love her, even if I didn't at the time. If I felt I *could* love the woman I was lying next to then it didn't matter if she was as ugly as a dustbin lid. For me to have a perfect sexual adventure with a woman there had to be a relationship first though — sex shouldn't precede the relationship.

A man and a relationship make a woman good in bed — an accumulation of things which end in the sexual act. And you can't just isolate one incident and say, 'That was magic — that was bloody marvellous.' You can only look at the overall relationship, which is mutually controlled by outside stresses, by the influences on the two people. But I don't think there is any way a woman could ever be bad in bed if I was deeply attached to and deeply attracted to her because then being with her and lying close to her would be enough.

When you first meet a woman you can tell if there is a mutual attraction, but you can't tell if she will be good in bed. Nor should you be able to tell because surely that is the enjoyment — the mystery of finding out. I think *that* is the absolute turn on for me. I think anything that is overtly sexy, unless it fulfills your private fantasy about sex, is not sexy at all. I like a woman who hints at things rather than overstates them, who seems unobtainable — so that you could never imagine in a million years that you could ever get her into bed.

I am attracted to the kind of woman I married — which is the tall Anglo-Saxon type I like. I like their coolness, I like their humour, I like long legs. I like women of thirty-odd to early forties. They have got a grace which I admire in everybody — athletes, entertainers. Some people have it, other people don't. I think it's very rare — it's as rare in a woman as it is in a great athlete or a great entertainer. I think very few have it, but the ones who do are very pleasurable and they are the ones that really excite me.

Diana Rigg has got poise, grace and style. She is not some silly, giggly girl. There is an intelligence about her, a maturity that turns me on.

I am old-fashioned enough to believe that the most satisfying way to make sex is in what is now laughingly called the Missionary position — I can't think that with all the tricks that one might have developed there's anything basically more satisfying than that. If a woman wants something else specific in bed, then you will find out by trial and error, and that discovery is one of the deepest mysteries of sex. It needn't even be stated because you do know eventually with somebody you're relating to closely. Obviously I'm not referring to the quick release of a one night stand — I don't look for that.

Fundamentally I'd be better off with a dirty book in a toilet than with a one night stand. I would feel unsatisfied, slightly seedy — the worst feeling in the world. I would feel seedy because of the betrayal of my own attitudes and the exploitation of another human being. It's fairly revolting to me — not at all like sex ought to be. A one night stand is an expensive form of mastur- bation, a mutual wank which happens out of inevitability at the end of an evening. Of course it is very sad if one partner cons the other into going to bed, but usually both partners know it is a one night stand and isn't going to lead to anything else. You do find 'Heartbroken, Richmond' writing off to a magazine saying, 'I had this marvellous scene with a man but he's not phoned me since.' Well — silly cow — it's her fault for unloading it the first night if she wants a lasting relationship.

I think there is a lot of fantasy in love-making that is in the mind but not in the act itself. Most people are selfish in bed in the sense that they try to please *themselves.* I think a lot of women still lie back and think of England and a lot of men lie on top and think of something else.

HUGH HEFNER

'What makes a woman G.I.B?' The major sex organ is the brain — contrary to some other things you may have heard, and an awful lot of it has to do with that: it has to do with what you express to one another, obviously on the emotional level. That's what really makes the difference.

JILLY COOPER

Jilly Cooper told me she didn't like talking about sex, but finally agreed to do this interview. She talked to me at her home in Putney, over drinks. Jilly, in a pink halter necked dress — was alternately fluent and hesitant, frank and shy. Extremely charming, surprisingly maternal and encouraging about my work.

'Good in bed' is totally acquired — I don't think I'm marvellous now — but I was terrible to start off with. Sex, like oysters and all the nice things in life, was not very pleasant at first. The first kiss I ever had was disgusting. I was very old — 17 — and it was at the May Ball, under a tree. A ravishing undergraduate, who was gorgeous (and who I later fell in love with) kissed me. He was extremely sophisticated and he stuck his tongue in my mouth. I nearly threw up — all I could think of was those little bobbles underneath the tongue, which you see when you examine your tongue in the mirror. Oral sex — one was disgusted by the idea — and actually doing it was initially revolting. But it is like gin — you get used to it — and then you love it.

When I was a virgin I used to wonder about being good in bed. I didn't know whether I ought to talk or not. Then people went to bed with me and talked — so I discovered that talking in bed was alright. But you hear girls saying, 'My husband is awful because he talks in bed all the time.' Then again, a friend of mine (a very well known television producer) once told me that he is a great non-believer in the decibel fuck because he thinks that women who make an awful lot of noise in bed are actually not coming at all. And that they only scream because they have been *told* to scream — whereas silent breathing is far more preferable. And I think that is a marvellous theory.

People ought to teach one another about sex. My first lover didn't teach me anything he just went to bed with me. He said, 'I adore you in bed — but you're terribly lamb-like' and I cried. I think he meant that I just laid there, was sweet and touching, said, 'Darling I love you,' kissed him a lot but didn't actually *do* anything. I loved him enormously — but I didn't learn anything from him.

Leo has broken down every sexual barrier I've ever had. That's why he's the best person I've ever been to bed with. I always have pleasure with Leo. I don't remember a time when I didn't — ever, ever — and I think I could count our disasters in fifteen years on one hand, which I think is a marvellous record. Leo has broken down my main block about sex — I was too shy to ask for what I wanted in bed — but now I do say what I want. Although it has taken a long time because (a) I'm shy and (b) my upper-middle class background is a killer. It would be equally difficult if ever I got married again, or had a love affair — unless I met the man when I was pissed, had marvellous sex with him and the barriers were broken down that first time (I think you do try much harder at the beginning and everybody tries really hard the first time).

Women often lack the guts to ask for what they want in bed because they're subservient. The good person in bed creates an emotional atmosphere in which their partner is relaxed enough to ask for what they want or admit being unhappy or worried. But I think everybody is inclined to gloss sex over and not to have the guts to say, 'I'd like you to dress up as a vicar.' People should discuss what they want — early on in a relationship — because if you don't and if you suddenly, after five years, say 'That is repulsive,' or 'Why didn't you do such and such' — it's terrible.

I've had my disasters — but I don't (touch wood) think I've ever been a disaster to somebody I've cared about. I was always enthusiastic and if I love somebody I want to give a great deal to them. But going to bed with somebody you don't fancy is death. Occasionally the pressure of guilt about *not* going to bed with someone has been so strong that one has thought 'Oh hell — come on, let's go to bed. . .' — as a matter of guilt, hoping that it will be alright on the night. But it isn't — it's always disastrous because you don't really fancy the man. You don't have any sexual pleasure — it's hurried and you feel you haven't given any sexual pleasure — it was dry and awful and neither of you enjoyed it. Of course I am sure that a woman can be good in bed in a man's view, yet still not enjoy the sex. We are all actresses and everybody fakes now and again. Although fortunately (or unfortunately) I am married to someone who knows when I am faking — so I can't.

I would probably have to fake for the first few times with anyone else out of nervousness, politeness and good manners. And most women are very apologetic, lie back and think, 'Oh

101

God — poor Terence — he had better stop because this must be getting boring for him. What he is doing to me is so lovely — but he has been doing it for so long. If he has to go on for another five minutes to make it work for me it will be too much for him — so I had better pretend that I am coming now.' One really has to be rather placid, relax, wait, and just think, 'Let him go on until it gives me pleasure — then I will give him pleasure in return.'

But I am quite certain men do feel 'Oh Christ, how much longer do I have to go on screwing?' (or licking or whatever), 'until she has an orgasm'. *You* think, 'How boring for him, he must be thinking about the weather or the piece he is going to write the next day.' So you stop and do something else, which is a shame — because sex is really like climbing a mountain — it's very boring, and then suddenly it becomes very pleasurable. But I know myself that when I am doing something to give a man pleasure I sometimes think 'Oh God, how much longer am I going to have to go on doing this — how much longer, how much longer. . .' So if *I* feel that way, what is there to stop the man from feeling the same?

It's no good making love if you're tensed up — I don't think everyone HAS to do it fifteen times a week — I think that's a load of junk because everybody gets tired. On the other hand you shouldn't go too long without otherwise you get out of practice. You are good in bed if you recognise when you are both getting so tense from not having sex that you've got to have it. I am always intrigued by this longevity thing — sex always seems to last much longer than it actually does. Everyone keeps saying that they go on all night — but *I've* never gone on all night in my life. I am absolutely finished after a couple of hours maximum. I might wake up and do it again — and then wake up and do it again — but I certainly couldn't do it all night.

I think if you're married, or in a long term relationship, you move into an area of fantasy. You can get to a stage where you are turned on by stories. Leo might tell me what happened in an affair back in 1950 and I might be turned on, because it's a story — he is not comparing me to her. Otherwise if a man talks about other women to me — I don't want to know about him. That makes anybody bad in bed — that's the A1 turn off. Long before I'd ever been to bed with anyone — a girl called Jennifer said, 'Jilly, you've been talking about other men in front of poor

Christopher all evening and one must never discuss men with other men.' Also I would never talk about sex to a girlfriend or go into details of what we did. I might just say, 'God it was fantastic' or 'it wasn't fantastic.'

I think an awful lot of damage can be done in bed. Women can massacre men, can make them feel simply appalling, and men can do the same to women as well. And it's really like being an actor — people worry after the last bad performance, after a bad one night stand when the man doesn't come back again. He just lays the girl and goes off into the night and is never heard from again. All the man has to do is to say, 'That was one of the most fantastic lays I've ever had. God — you're marvellous. . . if I'm ever your way — please can we do it again? But I really ought to go back to my wife now.' That at least leaves a feeling that the evening was good and that it worked. I think making someone feel they were disastrous is the worst thing anyone can do, because bed is a totally vulnerable area for both men and women.

If I were asked for advice on being good in bed, I would say it is the same as giving a good party. You start by seeing that everybody is happy. You've got to hand round the drinks and see that the biscuits are circulating. That the right people are meeting the right people (like the right part of your anatomy meeting the right part of the other person's anatomy). You have to think about the other person's pleasure — then you will be pleased yourself and will become more relaxed. Ultimately I think one wants to give pleasure and if at the end of the evening you feel that you've given someone a really lovely time and that you've had a really lovely time, a stunning three or four hours of pleasure, it's like going to the theatre — it's something lovely. And afterwards you want people to leave saying it was a good party — that it was pleasurable. I think, in a way, it is a duty after you've been to bed with someone to make them feel it has been pleasurable. In the same way as you want people to leave saying 'It was a good party', one of the nicest things is if people say thank you afterwards. Ultimately it all boils down to kindness. And I think as you grow older, you take pleasure as it comes, and you are joyful if it is joyful.

PETER USTINOV

'What makes a woman G.I.B.?' Sex is a conversation carried out by other means. If you get on well out of bed, half the problems of bed are solved. Sex is good if you understand someone – not if you are just attracted to her physically and nothing else. I can't take a flip attitude to this subject – it's very serious.

BARBARA CARTLAND

Barbara Cartland invited me to do this interview at her house in Hertfordshire. At first, Miss Cartland was very icy. She launched into a monologue – I tried to cut in – but Miss Cartland obviously felt she had demolished the subject. Tea arrived with special honey cake and I tried to chat, while looking as virginal as possible. Then – and I don't know what secret button I accidentally pressed – Miss Cartland was suddenly transformed. It was as if a sheet of ice had suddenly slid from her face; she became warm and human, gave me advice about publishers, publisher's contracts, introductions to six or seven of her friends and was genuinely kind to me.

Sex has become so vulgar and commercialised now people talk about being good or bad in bed – bringing it down to the lowest possible level and making it like a game of billiards or ping pong. People don't realise that everything has altered so enormously today. They have lost their sense of proportion and we have to realise that 'good in bed' is an entirely modern way of talking about relationships between men and women.

When I was young we were all very innocent – there was no question of good or bad – you didn't have to fight for your virtue because nobody attacked it. There was an enormous gap between the lady and the prostitute. Men would take a girl like myself out dancing and would never think of suggesting anything improper. They took one out because they admired you. They fell in love with you and wanted to marry you.

After the First World War – every man's idea of bliss was to come home – settle down with a house, a wife and have a family. That was spoilt a little bit later on because men didn't have the money to get married. In the meantime girls got more promiscuous simply because contraception was easy and they weren't likely to have a baby every time they were touched. In 1926,

a doctor lecturing at Oxford University told the undergraduates
that no woman was capable of feeling passion. Today we know
that women are just as capable of feeling passion as a man — but
its an emotional exercise as well.

I feel very, very sorry for the girls today because I think they
are often put in an impossible position and so have a very miserable time. But some girls are very stupid — they think that because
they go out to dine and dance with a man they *must* go to bed
with him. That's a very cheap form of prostitution. It's also very
degrading for the girl and they don't understand how much they
are damaging their characters and personalities.

Every man has been brought up with the idea that decent
women don't pop in and out of bed; he has always been told by
his mother that 'nice girls don't'. He finds, of course, when he gets
older that this may be untrue — but only in a certain section of
society. The great majority of people in England and America
are modest, decent and pure-minded and the amount of virgins in
the world today is stupendous.

The romantic age has come in — as I know from my books (all
my heroines are virgins until the ring is on their finger). I am quite
certain that in five or ten years it will be smart to be a virgin. There
has been an investigation just finished in America in which they
have found that where a woman is a virgin when she marries, the
marriage lasts longer and is much happier.

I don't think the man needs to be a virgin. There are always
divorcees and older women ready to make themselves very
pleasant to young men so a man can always find someone
experienced to teach him about sex. And I think that usually an
older woman does it very well. It's absolute rubbish, medically
and from any other point of view to talk about a man and a
woman being equal when it comes to sex. They are certainly not
equal. A man can have an 'affair' which can mean absolutely
nothing to him. He need never think of it again. It's the same as
having a good meal; it's an entirely physical reaction. But that
never, never, happens with a woman. For a woman, going to bed
with a man is always an emotional experience and therefore, it
affects her whole character. To sleep around is absolutely wrong
for a woman; it's degrading and it completely ruins her personality. Sooner or later it will destroy all that is feminine and
beautiful and idealistic in her.

105

Married life all over the world is being ruined nowadays because we have these women arriving with their sex manuals, saying, 'I am entitled to this, and why aren't we doing that?' That's wrong. In marriage it's a question of two people understanding each other and loving each other enough, not of following sex manuals. If the man loves the woman he won't do anything to shock her, and any man who takes a virgin wife to bed and frightens her is a brute. He is also not really in love. If a man loves a woman the one thing he will want to do is to make her happy and gradually make her desire him as he desires her.

If you love someone you want to make them happy – and if certain things make them happy – well then you do them – whatever they may be. There is no question of anything being wrong or indecent or improper if people really love each other. It is only wrong, indecent or improper when it's either done for money or merely for excitement, as a kick, not because one really is in love.

A woman asking 'Am *I* good? Am I satisfied?' is extremely selfish. The less women fuss about themselves, the less they talk to other women, the more they try to please their husbands, the happier the marriage is going to be. Men are frightened of these modern women who walk around with preconceived ideas of what must happen in bed. Making men feel that they must indulge in all sorts of peculiar things which they don't want to do. What is more, men nowadays are terrified that they will fail the false unnatural standards set by sex magazines.

A woman should say,; 'Have I made *him* happy? Is *he* satisfied? Does he love me more than he loved me before? Is he likely to go to bed with another woman?' If he does, then it's the wife's fault because she is not trying to make him happy.

My advice to women is make your husband happy, never mind what you feel. And, if he is trying to do the same, then everything is perfect. The only way a woman can judge if she's a successful wife is if she makes her husband happy. If a woman reads every sex manual in the world she still may not find what suits the particular person she is in love with and who loves her.

A man will teach his wife what is needed to arouse his desires. and there is no reason for a woman to know any more than what her husband is prepared to teach her. If she gets married knowing far too much about what she wants and doesn't want then she will be ready to find fault with her husband.

What is the point in wrecking a marriage from the very, very beginning by having preconceived ideas of what is right and what is wrong, or what is good or what is bad in bed? Ideas which may not be realized at first, but which with love, tenderness, gentleness and understanding, can in time become the foundation of a happiness which is perfect because it is shared.

That after all is the whole crux of the matter; sex — whatever form it takes — must be both physically and spiritually perfect for both the husband and the wife, remembering that love is part of the Divine.

BOB GUCCIONE

'What makes a woman G.I.B?' Sexual satisfaction is a two-way thing. If I went to bed with a woman who turned me on, whom I admired, but who wasn't really very good, I would *make* her good by virtue of the integrity of my feelings, my own needs, and my interest. That interest helps me to know the kind of woman I am in bed with; then I know how to direct my efforts.

You have to penetrate a woman's defences. Getting into her head is a prerequisite to getting into her body. Once I get her into bed, I do everything, say everything, and act in every way according to my particular sensitivity — my ability to understand what that woman wants and what she needs. Fulfilling the needs of the woman he is in bed with makes a *man* good in bed. If I were asked for a one line answer to the question 'What makes a woman good in bed?' I would say, 'A man who is good in bed'.

KENNETH TYNAN

Tynan: I've been monogamous for the last twelve years — so I'm really the last person to talk to about sex.

Wendy: But — 'Oh Calcutta'?. . .

Tynan: Oh well — that was all vicarious.

Wendy: That's what I say to everyone about this book as well.

Tynan: In my case it happens to be fact.

107

This interview was done at Kenneth Tynan's house in South Kensington after he had finished watching the Test Match on television. Later Kathleen Tynan joined us — first we discussed 'Carte Blanche' — and then — the intricacies of crotch-watching.

I am 49 now and over the years I have come to specialise. In the past I shopped around a lot but once you specialise you know what you want and what you're good for and then you tend not to diverge from it. But what I have always liked in bed is a girl with a beautiful bottom, an open mind, plenty of time to spare and some acting ability, an interest in sex outside bed as well as in, someone who is interested in words as well as deeds. I find words very sexy and tones of voice — so I like a girl with a sexy voice and an imaginative vocabulary. I don't mean I would want to sit and tell pornographic stories all night — it's just that the combination of words and acting can be that bit more exciting.

I've never been attracted to bright blondes and there's not one model in 'Vogue' or 'Harper's' featured over the last ten years that I've been attracted to (with the constant and permanent exception of Penelope Tree). All those stick insects swarthed in *tulle* . . . But the ideal woman for me would not be very muscular either. She would have unassertive breasts, a firm deep-clefted but not too flabby bottom and would be the sort of girl who would wear stockings and suspenders but never tights. She would have a sly, intelligent look and would probably not be a big extrovert. I prefer the cool approach. An over-enthusiastic woman — screeching and leaping about turns me off.

In my early days dark-haired Jewish girls were most likely to be good — well brought up Jewish girls — my first wife was a Jewish girl. I've also had great pleasure in the company of former convent schoolgirls — they were often magnificent sexual partners for me. Girls who go to those convent schools which, from the moment you enter the place, try to chase all thoughts of sex from your mind and of course succeed in filling your mind with nothing-else. Just because convent schoolgirls have been told all forms of sex are bad — they tend to think that all forms of sex are good. They are absolutely bubbling over with sexual fantasies just because they have been told not to have any. This makes them far more suggestible and far more capable of experimenting and far more open-minded than those girls who have been brought up permissively because girls like that tend, by the age of 18, to be totally bored by the idea of sex. A girl who has been brought up very freely has read all the books, and knows about everything from having it off with Alsatian dogs to going down on the Eiffel Tower — everything is *passé* to her. But to the convent schoolgirl sex is all deliciously new. And I also think that a well-developed and carefully nurtured sense of guilt can add a lot of pleasure to sex. The sense of doing something slightly *outré*. Because when everything is permitted then really very little is worth doing.

I find English girls are good but I've never been very excited by girls from the Mediterranean Catholic countries. It may, of course, be a language thing — because, as I've said, words matter to me a lot. French girls also attract me, because I speak French fairly fluently and so I can chat them up on the way to bed and in bed. The ideal woman for me has got to be pretty intelligent. The last thing in bed that would interest me (and I would yawn myself to sleep with) is a pretty girl without a mind or a sense of humour, that would be impossible. That's why I've never in my life gone to bed with a whore — because if there's no communication and intellectual contact I am just bored to death.

The woman who is good in bed has to share certain preferences I have. For instance, if her sexual fixation, apart from fucking, is with her breasts she is not going to get very far with me. I have never shared the slightly infantile taste for the breasts — I think they are very pleasant but I don't get wildly aroused by them. If a girl is in any way embarrassed by her behind then I am not going to be her guy. An awful lot of girls have guilt about their bottoms and any girls who have that had better not go to bed with me because they are going to be very, very embarrassed. Because I am a primitive who is much more attracted by the bottom — which is of course how animals always make love — the female presents her bottom. I don't mean anal sex — but I fuck in any position and bottoms do attract me enormously.

I would not be for any girl who is terribly into oral sex because I am not wildly into it myself. There are also certain physical things that turn me off. For instance if I am asked to perform cunnilingus with a giant cunt I can't do it and I don't blame myself for that. Also if a woman leaps on me and expects me to perform like an Olympic athlete — I would call that a cockcrinkler. There is no possibility of any performing in the presence of a lady like that. I do not enjoy and never have enjoyed, either on stage, or screen, or in my own life, heavy-breathing, athletic, gymnastic, cross-country-running, steeplechasing kind of sex, because I am not an athlete in any sense of the word. I am, in the words of a classic Mae West song, a guy who takes his time. It isn't that I *need* a long time − it's just that I like sex to *go on* for a long time and I don't subscribe to the wham-bang syndrome. H. G. Wells once said, 'Permit the song of Pan to be sung and it will be demanded with variations.' Well − I like the song − but I also like the variations, and I don't think there is one ideal way of achieving sexual union through sex. I like the by-ways. I like game-playing sex, role-playing sex − as well as person to person sex. I like silent sex, talking sex, acting sex and I also like living sex outside the bedroom. Playing games at parties, in railway trains, and in cars. There are a great many things one can do in cars on a motorway − *you* would be astonished and *I* would probably be arrested . . . And the woman who is good suggests her own scenes − you infect each other with ideas. There are little scenes one can act out -- there are games one can play and all sorts of free-wheeling variations − I don't think there is a platonically perfect fuck that we should all be aiming at and I don't like to approach sex in a spirit of holy reverence.

I think earlier in this century, when people were trying to get past the censorship barriers, they had to say 'sex is a holy matter − it was made in Heaven − and the contact of two bodies is like the contact of two souls'. D. H. Lawrence in *Lady Chatterley's Lover* does write about sex as if it were the next thing to Communion. Lawrence pitches the whole thing two octaves too high and starts to play the organ. Whereas he might have been just as satisfied by the mouthorgan − and *his* organ carries a cathedral around with it. But I was still turned on by some of the love making in *Lady Chatterley's Lover*. Also by a lot of French pornography from the 1920s and 1930s which turns me on − it's rather cool and discreet.

I find American pornography a dead loss because I find the language vulgar and crude. Also the subject matter is generally oral sex or masochistic men being dominated by whip-wielding women in leather boots − neither of which turns me on at all. But like many of my generation I was turned on by the Hollywood movies of the 40s. What was so sexy about those Hollywood movies was that they were never *allowed* to be sexy, so you had to read between the lines, and, if a girl crossed her legs and you heard the silk stockings swish, that would be very sexy indeed because you would be asking yourself if she was wearing knickers or not. So nudity isn't the only way to turn on (even though one can't be wholly turned on without total nudity). In a show like *Oh Calcutta* we had to be very careful not to lay too much stress on it. In any case, in *Oh Calcutta* we dealt only with the hetero-sexual whereas in *Carte Blanche* we deal with all the variations as well.

Nowadays anything which is a variation on the perfect genital orgasm (which everyone is after) is considered to be a heretic deviation. I find that a lot of people who are into Reich and Freud regard any kind of sexual game playing almost as the Catholic Church in the Middle Ages regarded heresy — as something to be stamped out. Absolute nonsense. I find that more American girls are like that but European people are less into the analytical scene, have not been so influenced by it and are not looking for perfect, Holy, sexual sacrament every time they hop into bed.

The woman's orgasm has become too much of a concern. Obviously it's better from both points of view if the woman comes. Just as it is better from both points of view if the man comes as well. But I don't think they must both come in the same, divine, melting moment. They each can come separately and then start again in reverse order. If the woman comes quickly — fine — that doesn't really worry me — women who come quickly seem to be able to come more often.

Sexual liberty has affected some women badly; at the height of the Swinging London scene, a girl told me that sexual liberty had been very bad for her. She said, 'I have been to bed with about 150 guys in the last three years and I've only had about four orgasms. Because nowadays if a guy says, 'Let's go to bed' and you refuse — he'll say, 'Fine' and just pass on to some other chick and make it with her within ten minutes. So you have to say yes — otherwise you miss out.' And this girl said she was constantly being left high and dry — or low and dry — . She found that sexual liberty only really existed for stud males and that it was not helping women to enjoy themselves at all.

You've got to make sure that the woman you are with is going

111

to enjoy everything that you do — and that you are going to enjoy everything that she does. I don't think there's any point in pretending you get an enormous kick out of something that you don't — there's never any point, especially after you are beyond a certain age, in too much sexual pretence. So if a woman refuses something I want in bed she is not less good — just a different type — chemically the wrong mixture. The two chemicals don't make the right combustion — that's all — and it doesn't mean that I'm wrong or that she's wrong.

Too many girls seem to think that they fail as human beings if they don't satisfy every man they go to bed with. That's ludicrous. A woman can't be all things to all men — nobody can — just as no man can be all things to all women. We are all different and I think the worst thing in the world is the girl who feels guilty because she doesn't satisfy every man — why should you? Of course if you have a bad night with someone you are in love with, you think, 'My God — here I am on top of the world, and I've let the world down.' But if you have a bad night with someone you aren't in love with then it doesn't matter so much. Most of us spend most of our lives on sex without love and people who say you've got to have sex *with* love are like people who say you must only travel by Concorde.

The woman who wants to be good should specialise — should find what she wants most of all in her secret heart and go for the man who wants that most of all too. I think when you are about 25 and have had some sexual experience, you should sit down and make a list of the psychological and physical attributes that attract you and simply look for those. And ask yourself, 'What do I honestly like? What am I honestly good at giving pleasure with?' Don't play the field — it's like being a cricket player; say you are a very good batsman, it doesn't mean you have to be a great fieldsman, a great bowler and a great wicket-keeper as well.

Everyone should specialise, should find out which particular sexual experience they want and find the partner whose pleasures match their own. It may be that your perfect sexual experience would be to dress up as the Pope and be fucked by a Cardinal (that's an extreme example). But everyone has desires that they never, or rarely, admit to themselves. The thing is to admit them as soon as possible and then go after them. Two people may find a total sexual truth through pretence, through acting — they may find something that is sexually magnetic and compelling but is based on a fantasy. So long as they think it is exciting and they are excited by it, who cares how they are excited. Don't be ashamed of your sexual desires, don't suppress them, don't hide them and don't, for God's sake, go into analysis and try and have them uprooted because that will only waste the best years of your life.

FRANÇOISE SAGAN

'What makes a woman G.I.B?' The best way to talk about love and sex is not to say anything about it — or just talk when you feel like it. Nowadays people talk too much about love and sex — the best way is to do it.

Sporting Life

JIMMY CONNORS

I once met Marjorie Wallace in Beverly Hills with a boyfriend
who kept calling her 'Miss World' — with pronounced irony.
Jimmy Connors, Marjorie's boyfriend at the time we met,
treated Marjie very differently — very lovingly and they both
laughed a lot together. Jimmy did this interview after prac-
ticing for a tennis tournament at Caesar's Palace, Las Vegas.
As Marjie introduced us, Jimmy was very relaxed, gentle and
unguarded. Before I left, he said: 'you can write anything
you want'. Nevertheless, this is exactly what Jimmy Connors
said.

I am pretty picky about ladies. Part of my pickiness is that I like
them not too skinny nor too fat — I like a little bit to hold on to.
My own pickiness is that I know what I like, but I can't tell if a
woman is good by just looking at her — only whether I want to get
her into bed. Looks can be very deceiving.

I don't like a woman who is loud, and I don't think I have ever
had a loud woman. I like sex very easy, no set times, no set anything. Timing is a very important word to me. Sex is no good if
one person likes it and the other person doesn't. I don't want a
lady who hits me with the headache ploy, 'I've got a headache; I
can't tonight.' There are some things you can get in the mood for
all the time, and sex is one of them, if it's with the right person.
I think feelings are very important. You don't have to be in love
with a woman, but feeling and enjoyment come into it very much,
even if it's just a one-night stand. Whatever the circumstances, I
don't think the woman would be there unless she wanted to be, or
unless she felt something in one way or another.

Faking is no good in bed. You do know if a woman is faking
in bed, I guess, by performance, because you know what the
feeling should be like on both parts. I guess a woman can say she's
had an orgasm, but she really hasn't, and I would hate to be faked
in that respect. I really would. That would be poor performance
on my part, wouldn't it? What am I there for? Am I there just for
my own satisfaction, or for both? Sex has to work both ways,
and I have to be with someone I really like.

I don't know if female athletes are better in bed. Athletics and
sports build one up and make one very firm. I don't know if I
want to say flexible, but I am not saying athletes aren't flexible,

117

and a lot of them are good in bed. I hate to get into chauvinism, but I don't think ladies are as strong as men, so athletics are tough on them mentally and physically. It's difficult for an athlete to have soft and smooth skin; it's tough on my skin. When you're out in the sun, it's tough on men, let alone ladies. For myself, I like ladies with very smooth, very soft skin I can nestle up to and cuddle with.

If I could choose the best woman in bed for me, I would like one lady, very soft, very smooth, very gentle, very cuddly, pinchable, squeezable, one that is very relaxed and very easy-going — Easy to be with — no pressure, either in bed or out. One that makes things easy for me — is equal, so that I am for her and she is for me. Above all, she must be a lady. I like ladies. I have always grown up to respect women, and you just treat them much different than you do men, in your attitude, in your tone of voice. Women, I guess, though, are a lot of people's downfall, and I am not going to say they are not mine. But I think behind every man there is a lady, and in my case it's off-court, and I need somebody there who is easy for me to be with, and easy for me to talk to, and doesn't just break my balls.

GEORGE FOREMAN

'What makes a woman G.I.B?' A woman is good if she is natural. Then she will naturally be good at whatever she does.

JAMES HUNT

At the exact moment that Richard Burton married Suzy Hunt — her ex-husband James was talking to me about what makes a woman good in bed. We started the interview as James drove me back from London airport where I had just met his plane from Malaga. The story that Burton and Suzy were about to marry had just broken. I had expected photographers at the airport — so had James and he seemed disappointed — and didn't mention Suzy throughout the entire evening. We did this interview at Peter Hunt's (James' brother's) flat in Battersea. As we walked in, I tore my Laura Ashley dress on the stairs, said rather ruefully that perhaps

I shouldn't have worn it — but James, very politely, said he liked long dresses. James Hunt has perfect manners, is very attractive, boyish and calls his brother 'dad'. James has struggled hard throughout his career, was very close to winning the title when we met and was obviously loving every minute of being the wild divorcee and potential champion.

If I could create the ideal woman in bed — there would probably be several hundred of her — in all different shapes and sizes to give me a bit of variety. All the nice things that women do in bed couldn't possibly be encompassed in one body, in one person.

Obviously — if a woman is very beautiful — with an outstanding body she *is* off to a very good start. But if she doesn't bother to use her body, or doesn't want to use it, or doesn't know how to use it — then she is not about to be any good. There are many reasons why a beautiful woman reacts that way; it could be that she's had too much sex and has got bored with it. It could be that she is too 'into' herself — and too bigheaded to get into sex. Sometimes beautiful women are inhibited in bed because they want to remain beautiful and serene — because they think they are better off like that. Beautiful women want to keep their movements beautiful and smooth and do all the right things in bed — so they give it too much thought and attention. They forget about what they are doing and they go cold, because they are not concentrating on the issue. Then you have to talk to them and make sure they come round and realise the folly of their ways.

Communication matters in bed, you can't do it in silence (well you can, but it's not much fun). I particularly like a woman who I can talk to and who can talk on my level. In that way you soon communicate what you want and what you want to do. Occasionally I've analysed myself when I am trying to manoeuvre a bird into bed and I quite amaze myself at how devious I am. Just setting people up. It's rather fun, it's the same business as selling. If you want to get something out of someone you've got to set them up to get it. So you lead them down the path they want to be led down — and that path eventually leads to wherever you want to get them. Sometimes you get a woman who will refuse something in bed because she is inhibited, or because she is frightened that she may like it too much. So then it's a matter

119

of relaxing her, working on her in subtle, devious ways, explaining to her that it might be a good idea.

But if a woman doesn't like something – why the hell should she do it? Refusing something she doesn't like doesn't make a woman bad in bed. But there are some women who make fake refusals. They do a number on you – refuse to go to bed for the sake of form – that's just a waste of time. Or they refuse to do certain things in bed and hold out to try and make an impression. But I don't believe that does anything at all. If you want it really chauvinistic, all they do is usually miss their fucking chance.

As long as the woman is trying then it's fine. The fact that she's trying is good because then she'll soon learn. A woman is better if she asks for what she wants in bed – I tell her to ask. The main pleasure, the main kick I get from a woman is really giving her a good time. I really like the birds to get in there and really enjoy it and if she is really, genuinely enjoying it that's the hell of a kick for a man, to be enjoyed. So If a woman wants something particular and doesn't ask for it – what am I supposed to do? Am I supposed to read her mind and guess? So I always like a woman to ask for what she wants and do it.

I prefer a woman who comes quickly because it's easier. It also means she is enjoying herself – enjoyment means orgasms, lots of them. And it's very difficult to make love to a woman who doesn't come at all. Particularly if you know she isn't going to come, because then you feel like you're having a wank. I mean the whole thing becomes slightly ridiculous. You are better off to have a wank. But I'd want to know why the woman hadn't had an orgasm because there's obviously something wrong if she knows what she is doing but can't come. So I'd be extremely worried and concerned on her behalf, because I would feel that she was losing out on the best bit. And I can't see anybody missing out on the best bit by choice. So I try and help – try and find out *why* she hasn't come.

If a woman doesn't come, 99 times out 100 it's because she has got the brakes on – because she's frightened to let herself go. An orgasm means that you get out of control, that's the whole fun of it, but some women can't handle that. So they go up and up – and then suddenly they'll stop – just when they should be coming. Or sometimes a woman doesn't come because she thinks that if she has an orgasm she is going to fall head over heels in

120

love with you, which could happen, which *does* happen sometimes, and is always a difficult situation.

There are plenty of birds. But even so some are memorable. I
think French girls are very well trained by their upbringing on how
to treat a man, how to make him feel good, how to appreciate
him and how to make the best of themselves. Though I don't
think French girls have more skill than most. Skill and experience
don't necessarily make a woman memorable in bed. I remember
a bird from a long time ago who was very young, very shy, very
sheltered. She was also very beautiful and she couldn't handle
being beautiful at all, was terrified of everybody. But I was nice to
her, talked nicely and formed a nice friendship with her. After
that, years of frustration and fear with men went out of the
window and she was a bombshell — because it was all bottled up
inside. That made her memorable.

Most women are more memorable for their personalities than
they are for their sexual performances. They range from somebody who is very compatible to you mentally and very much on
your wavelength, to somebody who's right out of your bracket
completely and very exciting because of that. Sex is also much
better if you are really flipped out on a bird. It gives it a lot extra.

If you are flipped out on somebody then the technicalities
and the skill of the thing don't matter — because you don't
notice.

Ultimately what makes a woman good in bed is the ability to
enjoy herself. The secret of success in bed is for the two parties
to have a jolly good time because that's what you go to bed with
somebody else for.

GEORGE SEGAL

'What makes a woman G.I.B?' A man makes a woman good in
bed — the one who is right.

GEORGE BEST

I interviewed George Best while he was in Los Angeles playing for the Aztecs. At the time, he was living very peacefully
in a beach house, reading 'Helter Skelter' (an account of the

Charles Manson trial), and did the entire interview dressed
only in a beach towel. I didn't feel shy or turned-on when I
realised — because he looked remarkably young and made me
feel maternal — a role for which George Best's image had left
me unprepared.

Fifty percent of the time I am with a woman who is good in bed.
Being a professional sportsman, I get groupies like entertainers do,
but eventually I get fed up. I have now gotten to the stage where
I'd rather spend time in bed with a girl who has a bit more intelligence — not just looks. Looks aren't that important to me now.
They were when I was younger and liked to be seen with a beautiful woman. But now, that is not that important to me. Looks
don't show whether a girl is good in bed or not. I know you've
got to get into bed with a girl before you can find out if she is
good because I have looked at girls and thought they would be
good, but have been disappointed, and vice versa.

So I don't believe there are any visible signs out of bed that the
woman is either good or bad. You just have to go on and do it.
Usually, though, the exhibitionistic type of girl is not very good in
bed, and the quieter type is better. So in a club or a bar I am
always more attracted to the girl who just sits there. I suppose it's
just ego, because the girl sitting there not smiling presents a challenge. It may be harder to attract her. In Los Angeles, things are
different. As no one knows me here, it's lovely — I have to do
everything on my own merit, whereas in England, it was easy to
find girls.

If I were Frankenstein, able to create the ideal woman in bed,
or if I could pick any woman in the world to go to bed with, I
would want Sarah Miles. Judging by what I've seen and read of
her, I think she's a beautiful woman — very talented, and also very
intelligent. What more do you want? But, then again, I change.
Next month it might be someone else. Otherwise I would like a
gymnast; the outdoor athletic type appeals to most men, I think.
There is something really beautiful about a woman with an
unbelievable shape, who is fit, fresh, healthy, and looks good. I
like an outdoor type of girl: blonde hair with natural looks,
like the beach girls you get down here in Redondo Beach where I
live.

I had the choice of staying anywhere in Los Angeles and picked

Redondo Beach. Originally I was going to stay in Beverly Hills, but I think that in the last couple of years, I myself have changed, and I would much rather be down here at the beach, where it's not as false. If I want to spend a couple of days in Beverly Hills, I can, but I couldn't live in a place like that. I find it false. Actresses and models — I can't stand the crap they come out with: 'Where were you born?' and, 'What is your birth sign?' It's all such a load of shit. It really turns me off.

I also get turned off if a woman needs a drink *before* she goes to bed. That kind of woman is bad in bed. So is the woman who says, 'I've got to have a smoke first.' It implies that she can't do without help from outside sources, and that turns me off completely. Some women have got to a stage of thinking they need it, and I don't agree with that. If a man is good enough, and the woman wants to be with him enough, then she shouldn't need any stimulation. I don't smoke marijuana at all. It doesn't interest me. I've never tried it, and I never want to try it. Maybe I am an outsider looking in. I know you shouldn't knock something without trying it, but I do knock it, and that is a big thing I've got against some women — if they can't go to bed without smoking.

Good sex has definitely to do with the atmosphere between you. If a man feels it's too much of an effort to make a woman come, that's laziness. If the evening or the time is right, then it will never take a woman long to come. But if she does take a long time, it doesn't really matter.

As far as I am concerned, head is not that important. It is *not* vital. I think head is more sex than actually being good in bed. There's a hell of a difference between being good in bed and being able to give head properly. A woman can be good at giving head in a car, or anywhere else, but not be good in bed.

A woman has to use her best attributes. I think the nicest thing is a woman who knows the sort of mood you're in, instinctively. It's nice on some nights, when I've been playing a game which hasn't gone well for me, to come home to a woman, have a couple of glasses of wine, and go to bed. Then, on nights like that, I don't want to have sex. I think a woman who is good realizes that and isn't selfish, because she knows you can make up for it other nights.

Everybody has off days — men as well as women. I have refused things in bed and so have women I've been with. But if a woman

123

doesn't feel like doing something I want in bed, I try very hard to change her mind. If she *still* doesn't feel like it, I just go to sleep.

DAVID NIVEN

'What makes a woman G.I.B?' To be on the same wavelength as the man she is in bed with, whatever that wavelength may be.

Couples

ROD STEIGER

'What makes a woman G.I.B?' Her love and knowledge that she is one-half of what she is going to make happy.

JANE BIRKIN AND SERGE GAINSBOURG

Wendy: 'You've made the ultimate orgasm record'.
Jane:　'What *do* you mean?'
Wendy: 'Je t'aime moi non plus'.
Jane:　'Oh – I thought you meant me *personally*'.

Jane Birkin and Serge Gainsbourg live in a little house on the left bank of Paris. I talked to them both there. Serge is often described as Jane's Svengali – who transformed an English rose into a sexy singer and film star. But instead of being Svengali-like, I found Serge very quiet and during the interview Jane dealt with her own business phone calls herself with great efficiency. Jane looks unchanged since she appeared in the 1967 film 'Blow Up'. She is now 29 and has had great success in France as a singer and film star. Serge has directed her in the controversial pornographic film 'Je t'aime moi non plus' in which she is sodomised by Joe D'Allesandrio. Jane told me she had changed radically in terms of her own sexuality since she left England. I said I wondered if perhaps the atmosphere of England was less conducive to being G.I.B. Jane said no – but that being away from home had uninhibited her. I agreed and said it had had the same effect on me.

JANE BIRKIN

Most people believe that our record 'Je t'aime moi non plus' was made while Serge and I were having sex. In fact it was recorded at Philips studios Marble Arch and Serge always said that if the record *had* been made by putting a microphone under our bed, a 45 would have been too short. Because of course I've had to confront taking a long time to come, just like other women so we would have needed to make an LP. . .

When I first had sex I thought I was terrible and I probably *was* a washout. I was brought up in England to firmly believe that

127

you shouldn't be easy, that you should keep your virginity for somebody special, so I stayed a virgin until I met the person I married, John Barry. Before that I didn't want people to talk about me behind my back and say, 'I've had her'. I used to hear about girls who were marvellous in bed, fantastic, and I would feel catty about them because they tended to be girls who (people said) had slept with half of London. I thought those girls were really cheap and easy 'they'll sleep with anybody, they must have lots of experience, so *of course* they will be getting good'. I believed that being good in bed just meant being experienced.

When I finally went to bed I don't think I realised that anything was expected of me. I just thought you got into bed, and then you just let everything happen. Sex went wrong for me all the time and must have been so boring for the men I was with. They were too kind to make me feel bad in bed but in retrospect I can see I was not very interested in sex, there was no complicity and I just sort of lay down. I thought, 'If this is all there is to sex then I don't know why everyone has built it up all that much'. Perhaps I was just too young.

When things went wrong in bed I envied all those girls who were supposed to be fantastically good. I thought, 'They seem to have everything — they can sleep with everybody and people take their hats off to them and say they are good in bed. Instead of calling them cheap and easy like they used to.' Leaving England made sex work for me — not living in one's own country changes things. I suppose it was only after I got divorced and started to live myself that I suddenly realised what being good in bed was. For me good was thanks to being with somebody special. Good in bed depends on who you are with. I can't imagine leaping on somebody in the street and being good.

Imagination makes a woman good in bed. A lot of women have got it but are a bit scared to ask for the things they have imagined. I was lucky enough to find somebody who had imagination and the same ideas as I had and didn't think I was stupid. Otherwise I don't think I would have had the courage to jump on someone and say, 'I've always wanted to see what it would be like to have it off in the bathroom.' It would have looked planned and you can't wait behind the door... Having sex in different places always interested me — although Serge isn't particularly interested in places.

I read quite a lot about sex theory. I read in a magazine about the Kegel exercises to develop the vaginal muscles. I thought, 'Hello, what's this. . .?' but I found them extremely easy to do. I tried the Japanese wa wa balls but I lost them. I thought they were somewhere near my throat (you know so little about that sort of thing) and the terror of getting them lost was a nightmare — I lost all trace. The wa wa balls didn't do the slightest thing to me so I thought, 'Those Japanese women just have got something on us — something must be different.' I also used one of those vibrators you massage your head with. Vibrators are so incredibly strong but I think they probably ruin you in the long run. They have the same danger of always doing something in exactly the same way — other things begin not to excite you as much. Also I think vibrator noise is about the boringest thing — it makes you want to laugh. Or makes the man laugh. (I always hope that if I sleep with someone he has got a sense of humour but doesn't laugh at the wrong moment). Really though, I always think vibrators are a bit rough on the man. They have the same effect as if he suddenly produced an envelope and fiddled around with it, while touching you. You would then think, 'Oh dear, perhaps the envelope has got something over me. . .'

In the past I faked orgasm because of feeling inadequate — because I didn't want to hurt someone. It's awful if a man asks if you have come and you haven't. If you say no it makes *him* look as if *he* is bad in bed then he gets worried. So you lie to him — but you never really lie to yourself. You start to worry so much, you feel inadequate and not having the orgasm becomes a wall which you build up. I think it gets easier to have orgasms as you get older — but until then it can be a terrible problem — as I know it was to me.

I do think that to be good you should try everything and not put barriers up at once. If the person you're with is interested in something you might as well have a bash at it because you never know, it might interest you too. You should try and have as much imagination as the person you are with. Without rushing off and buying plastic macs. Even so — have one. . .

I don't think I have ever refused anything in bed — but then nothing suggested has been so terribly terrible. I don't see why one would say no to practically anything. But I can imagine refusing being chained up against a wall or other things that would

129

also hurt me and actually make me bleed. I also don't get turned on by other people watching me have sex. Serge has directed me in a hard-core porn film in which I was sodomised. I found it embarrassing being filmed like that, I don't like being naked, I don't feel comfortable being filmed with my legs open — I hate it. It makes my cry.

Orgies never interest me either. I have never been to an orgy or done group sex. Directly I see a party turning that way I leave — I think it is the most asexual thing in the world. On the other hand, I wouldn't mind peeping through a keyhole and watching somebody else do it. But I just want to be with one person and I wouldn't like the idea of somebody else touching him. I suppose you have to go to an orgy with somebody you don't care about — but then why be with them in the first place?

The best advice I can give on how to be good in bed is to remain a mistress. I have been with Serge for eight years and I think the greatest mistake in a long relationship is to become the wife. Because then the man will begin to respect you like a wife — and *that* kind of respect will eventually lead him to a prostitute. In fact, I think a woman should be a prostitute in bed. I think all women, at some time, have imagined being a prostitute — it's always been a rather nice idea. Of course you don't want to go through with it but you should be a prostitute for your man sometimes. Ask for money to be laid down sometimes, symbolically, it's quite important. And if the man wants to knock it off in four minutes flat, without thinking of you, you should let him do it. And he should be capable of doing the same for you — I think that can be quite exciting — being used — I don't see why one *shouldn't* be used occasionally — you can always get your own back. . .

Men like to surprise a woman sexually, the woman who is good doesn't look as if she is *always* waiting for sex. I think that makes men slightly sick. Don't get too worried if sex doesn't happen all the time because there are always ups and downs. Don't keep thinking about sex all the time because if men feel you are continually wanting sex and they are in a down period, they get fed up. Then they start getting complexes, they begin to feel impotent, as if *they* are bad in bed — and then they will never forgive you.

SERGE GAINSBOURG

The ideal woman in bed is unafraid of using all three orifices. She has variable types of orgasms, sometimes perfect, sometimes imperfect. She is mostly receptive, but sometimes unreceptive. She is depraved, sophisticated, is not afraid to use accessories, and to explore fetishes.

Sex is a question of affinity of the flesh — affinity or rejection. A woman can be nothing with one man, and the next day; fantastic with another, if there is affinity. And the day after she can be completely different if conditions change. If I were Doctor Frankenstein and able to create the ideal woman in bed, I would create Jane, because she is perfect sexually.

I don't like Olympic performances — for me love is a cocktail of the spiritual and the physical — half and half. If a woman looks extraordinary but I don't love her, the sex is boring and depressing for me. Without soul, sex is like an olympic performance or something in the sauna.

Bad in bed is frigidity — or non-receptiveness. However, a girl who is bad in bed can sometimes be interesting. If she is frigid she seems like an object or a plastic doll. And her frigidity can induce the girl to search for potential pleasures, and her search may transform her into a nymphomaniac.

It's sad if a woman doesn't have an orgasm, but if you don't love her — you don't mind and you just help yourself. Psychiatrists say that for a woman to have an orgasm she mustn't be afraid of death. If a woman is afraid of death, she won't have an orgasm. Because an orgasm is like an epileptic fit.

If a woman refuses certain things in bed it can be erotic. The idea of sin is erotic. Her refusal opens the door to eroticism, creates guilt. A psychological barrier against something sexual incites the man to rape the woman sexually, and that can be erotic.

I directed Jane in a pornographic film which goes beyond sex. In it she is sodomised by Joe D'allesandro. It is embarrassing for her — the lights, the cold floor. Joe was also embarrassed — but they were acting.

Jane: I don't like to be seen by somebody doing something to somebody else. I don't like being naked in front of the camera. I hate it — it makes me cry. For me it is like being on the gyne-

131

cologist's table. I don't like doing it, but it was necessary for the film.

Serge: I was very cold — because I was thinking about editing, music, worrying about the photography, so you are ten miles away from being sexually excited by the scene. I felt happy though, thinking that the scene would be erotic in the movie. But I also felt embarrassed and guilty. I think it is sad to see a girl you love become such an object.

ELKE SOMMER

'What makes a woman G.I.B?' Chemistry makes a woman good. If your knees shake when you see a guy, that's chemistry. After eleven years of marriage, instead of the knees shaking with a sense of novelty, you have a different feeling. It is not the heart fluttering any more. But you also don't need to perform any more either — you can relax and be yourself. You can be comfortable and not worry about your makeup and the way you look. If you are loved, then you have to be good in bed.

ALEXANDER THYNN, VISCOUNT WEYMOUTH

Alexander Thynn: 'Do the people you interview say fuck or copulate?'
Wendy: 'Either'.
Alexander: 'Well — I had better say both.'

I interviewed Lord Weymouth, heir to the Marquis of Bath, at his London flat. We talked for nearly two hours; he was hesitant, tentative, apologetic — and careful not to hurt my feelings. When I asked Alexander to describe the perfect woman in bed, he told me that my question was embarrassing: 'If I describe a type and it doesn't happen to be your type, it will be rather embarrassing. For example; you have medium length red-hair, but I am turned-on by waterfall tresses.' I reassured him, saying I wasn't there to be flattered, so he gave me his answer and then we went on to discuss Alexander's theories of polygamy: 'I expect all my women to be polyandrous. Once upon a time I felt a bit cheated because British culture led me to believe one was going to get a virgin wife and remain faithful. Then one was brought up in a state of divorce and discovered that what one had been led to expect was so different from the reality. That made me do a somersault. I didn't just react against it — I also wanted to put something in its place. So I evolved my theories, to be moral in my own way. I see the polymorphous society coming in — with the right of any individual to choose whatever family pattern he wants — under the umbrella of the state — with no questions asked. You could choose to be polyandrous, have a group marriage, or many couples might still choose to be monogamous. But if a woman truly wanted to be monogamous — I suspect that she wouldn't have a relationship with me.' We didn't directly discuss Lady Weymouth, who lives in Paris, nor the unconventionality of Lord Weymouth's marriage to her.

VISCOUNT WEYMOUTH

I am afraid I ought not to be talking as an all-knowing professional because I should be surprised if my total number of affairs would top the figure thirty. And that even includes one night affairs, which isn't much for a 44 year old.

When I first meet a woman, certain things trigger me. Visually I tend to like women with an air of mischievousness, the indication that we might have fun. I like well formed women of small build, with waterfall tresses. Eyes in which I can read a strong interest in me so that I feel the woman is trying to look into me — which in turn encourages me to look into her. There has got to be a spark that is played backwards and forwards. There has got to be a ping pong feeling that we're both in it, otherwise the sex is like watching a film. The game obviously stops though if the woman doesn't fancy me. Women have told me that they didn't fancy me and however truthfully or sophisticatedly it is done it still remains a very grim statement. There have been times when one has had a nice relationship with a woman and has gone to bed out of kindness because if one didn't it would have amounted to saying, 'I don't fancy you.'

Sympathetic, extroverted women make the first time you go to bed easier. I think the first time you make love to a woman is probably the most difficult love-making of all because of the nervousness and embarrassment. It is very important that verbal communication happens before bed — that one knows one is together sexually on certain levels.

An inclination towards experimentation makes a woman good — but I personally prefer it if the initiation comes from myself. I wouldn't downgrade a woman who asked for what she wanted but I like a woman who enables me to play through my culturally imposed male role. I have been brought up in the culture of the male setting the pace — rightly or wrongly. So that if I feel I am not initiating the relationship, that the woman is setting the pace, I feel emasculated and I might not even get an erection.

As long as the woman allows me to believe that I am giving her great pleasure, that I am actively initiating the relationship, it wouldn't matter if she had had more experience than I had had. It would matter, though, if she made me feel, 'Come to me my son — I'll teach you things,' because then I would also feel less masculine. Being good in bed might become a disadvantage for the woman if she displays tremendous sexual expertise, while pretending to be inexperienced and pure. I would feel deceived if a woman was presenting me with such a false image. Once I realised that there was trickery and falsity I would be turned off.

I am afraid simulation during love-making is one of the totally unmentionable subjects. If I realised that the woman had faked orgasm, I would never remark on it, but once I knew I'm afraid I would always think, 'Here goes the simulation.' But if the woman doesn't have an orgasm I don't think I ought to get uptight about it nor do I treat it as a failure in the love-making. Failure in bed comes from a frigidity about what sex is. The woman who is bad in bed might insist that sex has to be 'natural' — that nothing else is right, that one must always do the missionary position.

The woman who is good in bed is unshockable. But then again, there are things which *should* be shocking — like the Moors Murders. There has got to be a standard somewhere — so I would rather say that the woman who is good has a certain degree of unshockability. She is also active as opposed to passive. The woman who is good knows that the man will get pleasure from knowing she is pleased. And she has the ability to let him see that she is delighting in whatever is being done to her. A vast display of delight flatters the man into thinking that *he* is good in bed and I believe that that kind of ego satisfaction is important.

134

Beauty in one's bed — having a beautiful woman — also flatters one's ego. However, when one has had a relationship with a woman for a while and she has 'gone off' in looks — one knows perfectly well one can be just as happy in bed with her as when she had beauty. Anyway, I've also had women of lesser beauty and I haven't noticed a marked change of standards. But for the taking to bed, for the initiating of a relationship, beauty does matter because one likes to think of oneself as someone who has beautiful women in bed.

The prime factor that causes me to maintain my contact with women is not necessarily that they are good in bed. The first ingredient is that I find the relationship durable at other hours of the day and also the mental compatibility and the personality. Even if the sex is not the height of enjoyment one might have reached elsewhere I could forgive (as I hope the woman could forgive) a lot of deficiency in good in bed. But if the woman is good then that is a plus.

I like to be liked — I like it to be known that I am liking. I like to think most of my women are beautiful — and I like to think that they are good in bed.

LADY WEYMOUTH

Viscount Weymouth said he didn't think his wife would agree to be interviewed for this book — but she did and we met in Paris at La Coupole Restaurant. Hungarian born Lady Weymouth, who acts under the name of Anna Gael, is very beautiful, with long brown hair, grey green eyes, no make-up, natural and gentle and very much the modern, liberated woman.

Wendy: 'You asked me not to ask you about your marriage with Viscount Weymouth. But, your husband talked to me about polygamy — I know *I* would like to be polyandrous — but I also know I would find it difficult to have a relationship where the *man* was polygamous as well. Can I ask you how you cope?'

Lady Weymouth: 'I don't want to talk about my private life and I won't give you a straight answer. However, I can skirt around it and tell you that sometimes life puts you in a position where all you can do is lie low. Sometimes life is very cyclic — at times you have to lie low but you must not let the lying low periods destroy or demolish you. In every situation there is something that can make you richer and stronger. You have to find that by having your own beliefs in life. You have to put yourself in another person's shoes, and try to understand them and obviously you then become more generous in your attitude. So you lie low, you just observe and try and find as much comfort as you can. People who want, want, want out of life are people who are not sure of themselves. Once you have understood that, you can afford to be much more generous.'

I am a bad example because I practically never go to bed. I know that sounds crazy, yet I am a normal person — I don't have any biological troubles and I am not frigid. I just wish we could go back to the times when we could just let the feeling come and then have the body follow. It seemed much more natural because it's easy to satisfy the body, but the mind and the emotions are much more vulnerable. I have never ever bought this whole new thing of the man assuming that if you go out to dinner with him you will automatically also go to bed with him. I can't do that.

Before I go out to dinner with a man I say, 'You know I won't go to bed with you, do you still want to go to dinner with me?' I have been very lucky up to now — the men have still gone out with me. I can't believe men really *want* to go to bed so much — they just do it to prove that they can put a woman into their bed.

I sometimes say to my male friends, 'Listen, if I go to bed with you once — will it make things easier? Shall we be friends then? Will you leave me alone?' I actually did once — just to see — but unfortunately it doesn't stop anything — men have got to prove things to themselves again and again — so now I've stopped doing it. One is pressurised to go to bed the whole bloody time and I find it a pain in the neck. The times I do go to bed are very, very, very rare — then I feel like it. Sex is absolutely marvellous with love, marvellous with feeling, but I don't go to bed for sex's sake. I don't enjoy sex for sex's sake.

People have laughed at me and said, 'My poor Anna — you are so depassé,' but for me it is always sex for love. I don't play a part. Some people dare not show themselves as they really are. For example: I take the tube because I don't have enough money at the moment to take taxis — I think it's stupid, I'd rather spend my money on a nice pair of trousers than on six taxis. But the other day I met a girlfriend of mine, who is also an actress, on the tube. She was horrified and said, 'For God's sake don't tell anyone you've seen me on the tube.' Why not? People are not sincere, they play parts. If I did play the game I would only go out with men I fancied terribly, terribly, terribly and knew I would develop feeling for. After the third dinner I'd go to bed and hope that after the sixth I'd be in love. I believe very few women go to bed for sex's sake — only those who are made like men.

I agree with the ideas of Woman's Liberation but I am not a fanatical Women's Libber. I think women are getting the worst of both worlds at the moment. We have lost all the respect and consideration men had for us — which used to be very nice. Even male chauvinist pigs who never really respected women deep down, had a surface respect which made life much easier. They couldn't behave quite as outrageously to your face as they do now. Who has not been stood up? Who has not been telephoned after an evening in bed?

A girlfriend of mine was pregnant. She had been going out with this man — and had already booked herself in for an abortion. She didn't want any money from him, just a bit of sympathy. So in the middle of the night she cuddled him and said, 'I am pregnant but I am going to hospital for an abortion.' He looked at her and said, 'Scram, get out.' When she told me I really felt heart-broken. That is an example of what women have lost. Men treat us as if we are tougher than they are. My daughter will probably be better off. By the time she grows up equal pay and women not necessarily minding the baby, issues that make men itch, will be sorted out. And then perhaps men will also realise that because a woman is liberated she does not have to be treated as something as tough as iron.

Women also sometimes react to men as stereotypes. They have a tendency to treat them as if the men had something to prove sexually. I think a woman should treat a man with respect and be gentle with him. Give him something that is unheard of and that men rarely resist — tenderness. Treat him like a very fragile flower, not at all like a big he-man and he will be delighted. Give him warmth. I think warmth is the rarest quality in the world. So many people have diamonds yet so few have got warmth.

One of the big secrets of a relationship at the start is not to ask too much. If you are too demanding and ask too much for all the things you crave; to be taken into his arms and protected, he will be scared. But if you are a giver to start with then he won't be frightened and later on he too will give. Men are so used to being asked for things by women that now they have become so stingy about giving in the emotional sense.

I think that emotions are so fragile they have to be protected. I have been faced by the situation where a man has asked me to do something I didn't want in bed. I've always said no and I haven't lost the man. It was natural for me to say no, I *did* think there was a possibility of losing the man but I was prepared to accept it. It was somebody I was concerned about but I managed to skirt around the problem and never do anything sexually I didn't want. Even if I loved the man I wouldn't do something I disliked just to be good for him. I would think that I loved the wrong man and that he loved the wrong woman. Each individual has their own psychological and emotional pattern which is unique and can't be duplicated. It is absolutely no good to go against your pattern because otherwise sooner or later you will break.

I am too busy to play games – I can't be bothered to play the bitch. I think it's degrading. If I loved a man I always told him I loved him – if I was happy with what he did to me in bed I always told him and he seemed very pleased and came back. Of course you shouldn't tell a man you love him straight away. Love needn't be spoken, only after a long, long time. At the beginning it should always remain unspoken – but you can show the man that you care.

I suppose the women are right who say that a woman should not make herself too available to a man. Yet I manage otherwise. I manage by living my life to such an extent that of course I am not available all the time. If I had a choice I suppose I would be available more. One manages not to suffer because one keeps busy. But I have never ever pretended not to care about a man when I did.

I would fake in bed, though, if I were fed up with the whole performance. And why not if the only thing you want is for the sex to end? But as I only go to bed when I *really* want to – then on those times I don't *have* to fake. I don't think I would care very much if a man made me feel I was not up to standard. If he told me I was not good enough I would say, 'I am sorry, try somewhere else.' But if I loved that man I *would* be good enough. The whole point of love is that you adapt to the person you love. Love is giving before taking. So when you love you want to find out what the man wants, what he feels, so how *can* you be bad? And the man who feels that he is with a woman who is tender and indulgent, is natural and doesn't pretend, will let himself go. Whereas if the woman acts as if, 'I am the Queen, I am the best, you can't ever match me,' then all the man will do is try and give his best *performance*. He won't really *care*. Every love affair has its heartaches and if the man doesn't care you will be in pain. But if the man cares and wants you a lot it will be worth it. I think there is only one rule — to be as natural as possible. Be as rich a person as you can be. Live and live your life — build yourself into somebody who has as much inner richness as possible. And if you are a rich person — if you have enough to give, the man will respect you. He will say, 'She is clever, she is good looking, she leads an interesting life and she knows where she stands. She can't be swayed by the world of snobbery and fashion.' Then he will find you worth it, and like you so that you can go on. . .

RYAN O'NEAL

'What makes a woman G.I.B?' My father used to say there is only good and better.

VIDAL AND BEVERLY SASSOON

Vidal and Beverly Sassoon are Beverly Hills' beautiful couple. They now have a best-selling book 'A Year of Beauty and Health' — and when I met them were starring in their own T.V. show. The show's motto was, 'Look better, think better and feel better with the Sassoons' and they were their own best advertisement. Beverly, an ex-beauty queen and Hollywood starlet, demonstrated exercises and beauty tricks and Vidal interviewed celebrities and was notorious for forgetting their names. The Sassoons make the perfect couple — Beverly always beautiful — and Vidal quick, funny and sexy. I know

139

both of them well — and have never seen them eat anything remotely fattening — or look anything but perfect. And that means effort — even for the stunning Sassoons.

VIDAL SASSOON

Sex is perspiration and animation. I think that, above all, sex is an art form. We should have legalized sex houses. People should be able to go to good sex houses and learn about sex, in the same way as they are able to go to good restaurants and learn about food. Because the more you know about sex, the more exciting it becomes.

It is terribly important to help people over their sexual hangups and allow them to enjoy sex at the earliest age possible. When my son is fifteeen, I would like to hand him over to a superb courtesan to learn all about sex. I know he will find out eventually. I first had sex at seventeen. I was a late starter, but I still didn't find out what it was all about until my late twenties. Prostitutes were out of the question because everyone kidded that you would get some vile disease. Anyway, I was too proud to pay for sex. I don't want my son to go through all sorts of sexual nonsense, first, because although experimenting can be a lot of fun, a young man needs to develop a lot of expertise to increase his own confidence.

I also don't want my daughter to get screwed up. Screwed is okay, so if she asked my advice at sixteen or seventeen although I couldn't be her pimp I would hope to find a gentle and experienced man to take her into hand. A girl can really be tortured as a virgin, if her first sexual experience goes badly.

One of the worst things about sex is getting used to doing it with a woman in a set specific manner. But the woman who is good can really turn a man on to nuances and stir up his imagination and feelings, either with gentleness, words, physical things, or mood. She creates an excitement. A woman who is good in bed can 'get' to most men in the end. I used to work for Raymonde, the hairdresser, and he once said to me, 'If you are having caviar every night, occasionally it is very good to have fish and chips.' I think if a woman treats sex as an art form and is very explicit and innovative in the art of making love, then a man will stop looking for fish and chips and stick to caviar.

I truly think that over a long period of time, fit women are better in bed (a woman can have thick bones, yet have a muscular body with stamina). Over a long haul — a marvellous four-hour bash — the woman has to be fit, or else she is going to doze off exhausted after twenty minutes. There is a tremendous amount of physical exhaustion in sex at its best — not necessarily in acrobatics — but in the physical exertion and strength needed for good sex. Fit people are better at sex as long as they have everything else going for them, like desire and the urge, the appetite and the libido.

The thought of having sex with an older woman who has kept herself beautifully has always intrigued me. Ten years ago I saw Marlene Dietrich at Dior in Paris, and there was this most exotic woman. My fantasies run in that direction. Sex is a vibrant, youthful thing, done by people of all ages if they have kept themselves looking youthful and marvellous no matter what age they are. A sixty-year-old woman is good if she is experienced, but all a teenager needs are her youth and the charm of naivete, which turn a man on in bed.

I think hot-blooded women who make demands can be very exciting. If a woman refuses what I want in bed, then it is marvellous to be able to gently coerce her. It is a challenge, and I believe people need challenges in bed, except in new love, when everything is hot and the only thing one needs then is the moment in time. But in most sexual relationships, the more you have sex the more profound you become.

If a man is feeling strong and everything is going along nicely, and he is in full control (because it is sometimes nice to be in complete control) he won't mind the woman taking a long time to come. But there is something marvellous about a woman having half a dozen orgasms to the man's one. That gives him a tremendous sense of being superman, even if it is just for that evening. If a girl doesn't come the first time we go to bed, then it is a challenge, something to make work the second time. Rather like with the girl who doesn't open her legs the first time you go out with her — the whole thing becomes a challenge.

A woman has to be happy at making love. You can never force that happiness. Some women are slightly animalistic at making love, and for them sex is one of the greatest experiences of all time. Very few women are frigid with everyone; therefore, if a woman is bad in bed with you, it may be because you are not

141

turning her on, perhaps because the skin textures and the smells are incompatible.

If I were Frankenstein and able to create the ideal woman in bed, she would have Suzy Parker's legs and my wife Beverly's face. She would use her head in bed; sex is cerebral. If she had children and wasn't as tight as a virgin, she would use her legs and the muscles in her stomach and her back. Being good in bed is knowing what to do with what you have got.

I believe nothing is wrong in bed — nothing is bad. If you fail, you should just have a good laugh, because I think sex can be funny. Everybody, whoever they are, must have fouled up in bed once or twice. The grass is never really greener, because everyone has their problems, their off-days, and their marvellous days. No one is King Kong; there aren't any supermen or superwomen. so everyone should just view sex as something to look forward to; a super-plus.

BEVERLY SASSOON

I learned about sex through experience. I was sixteen, and my first boyfriend was very good and made the whole experience pleasant. Unfortunately, so many of us were raised with the approach that sex is taboo; but getting over that and attaining mental freedom makes a woman good.

I don't know if I project being good in bed. You can be that without appearing flashy and showing a lot of cleavage. When I look at a man I feel I can tell if he would be good for me — but I don't know if he can do the same about me.

I really believe sex is just for two people. Group sex or orgies are not my scene. No one has ever asked me to take part in anything like that, and I think I make it very obvious by my attitude that *that* is not where I am at. If I were asked, I would say, 'No' or, 'Thank you' or, 'Goodbye.' I have never ever been forced to do anything I didn't want in bed. I believe sex should be exciting and thrilling, but I don't need added attractions to improve it. I would never put myself into a situation with someone I didn't trust, or who didn't know what he was doing, and I would never let anyone intimidate me in bed in any way. For example, if someone was a celebrity or a big movie star, I would never let that intimidate me. There are a lot of people walking around the streets who are probably just as good, if not better, than a celebrity.

I don't think you need to *ask* for what you want in bed. I think if a woman has any sort of intelligence, she can lead a man into doing what she wants. I am not a big talker; I don't think it is necessary to talk a man into being excited; I think that can all be done without words. If a man is inexperienced, it is fairly easy to guide him.

The woman who is good makes the man feel sex is his whole responsibility, but doesn't necessarily leave it all totally up to him. He can *think* that he is taking all the initiative and doing wonderful, marvellous things on his own, whereas actually a lot of the initiative comes from the woman. That sounds a little deceitful, but it sometimes is necessary, although sex is not a game it has to be handled intelligently. I always need a fairly solid foundation with a man before we have sex, because I don't believe in jumping in and out of bed with different people.

I don't feel less good if I take a long time to come. The more time you can spend in bed, if you are enjoying sex, the better. Worrying sometimes prevents an orgasm, because you must relax and enjoy the moment. Then, if an orgasm still doesn't happen, it doesn't happen. There are times when people do ask you if you have come, which is a fair enough question, if they don't know. The best way to answer is to be honest, unless, of course, you feel the answer will completely crush the man.

There are times when I find that I am not physically interested in sex. My sexual desire is lessened when I feel that I am slightly overweight or when I see something about my body that I don't like. When I am really thin I feel terrific in bed. I am not saying that thin women are better in bed; it is just that I feel *I* am better when I am thin because when I am in good shape, and I feel attractive for myself. Then it follows that I feel attractive for the man. I also think it is very important to know one's own body just as well as one knows the man's body.

If I had to give another woman general advice on how to be good in bed, I would say that sex is like riding a horse. You must let the man have his head.

143

Stars of Stage and Screen

PAT PHEONIX

I had a terrible cold when I arrived at Pat Pheonix's cottage near Manchester. After the interview, Pat gave me dinner then packed me off to bed with an asprin. Everything was in true Elsie Tanner character — except, unpredictably, for Pat's graciousness. I also missed the Elsie Tanner in her voice, and when I told her, Pat obligingly talked 'Elsie' for me. Her then husband, Alan Browning, was away appearing in a play and Pat seemed very content, secure, almost serene. We talked about astrology, about her love for pets and about the effects of us both being only children. In the middle of the evening an ex-boyfriend phoned me at the cottage — and that led to Pat and I discussing our attitudes to men in great detail. Elsie Tanner and Pat Pheonix have different attitudes to men; Elsie, said Pat, thinks men are marvellous and loves them all. Whereas Pat's final advice to me was 'First, always believe in fairy stories, always believe in Prince Charming, always believe that this man is *it*. But still, always hold on to the other side of you that says, 'It can go wrong — and if it does — I will do this and that'.

I am not nearly as sexy as Elsie Tanner — she thinks all the fellas are lovely — I don't and I reckon I am lousy in bed. I have a strong maternal instinct which is, I think, very often mistaken for sexuality. I am lazy and languid — I always found acrobatics very boring — we rounder women are never so energetic in bed. I am selfish enough to like it when I like it — and I want to go to sleep when I want to go to sleep!

I went to an all-girls school, so sex was a great curiosity and a romantic dream for a long time — I only discovered where babies came from when I was nineteen. In my youth sex was not discussed openly or freely — only hinted at. The whole thing was like a thirties movie — all beautifully wrapped up. I had romantic fantasies about King Arthur and Robin Hood and all the film stars. I remember my actual thoughts about sex as strange, disturbing feelings that seemed wrong at the time. We were all guilt-ridden about sex, in the forties and fifties.

I always found that I never had any shortage of men in my life — simply because I was always running away from marriage. Marriage was a word I never mentioned. If a man did — terror —

I was up and away. So — for a plain woman — I did very well. In my youth, the busty, swinging girls were always considered very sexy. Later on I sometimes did have men make the effort to go to bed with me so they could simply say they had. The men *I* liked always had to be status symbols to *me*. I liked men with power — because then you possessed the brain of the man — and there is nothing better than to be seduced by a brain. A bit tricky of course...

I never had a short term relationship in my life. Never. They have always lasted for years. One lasted for nine years — when it was really over by the first year — I was afraid to hurt the man. One will always admit there are those firey moments when you will fall for a quick tumble. I've had a couple of one night stands in my time — for larks — and I made sure they were lovely and stayed just for laughs.

My first husband was eight years younger then me — and I felt the difference. I am always frightened by the idea of middle-aged women having relationships with young men. You see a woman go beserk over a man twenty years younger — he loves her for that moment — but a woman ages very quickly and it becomes pathetic. One of the emotions I have always detested is pity and I would hate to receive it. My first marriage broke up because things were asked of me sexually that I couldn't comply with. I always refused if I didn't want to do something — it's a question of survival — of your self-respect.

Memory lasts a long time and you must try never to do anything you're going to regret. Once a man asked me to an orgy. In those days, I didn't know what an orgy was — I just thought it was something where you all ran around in cami-knickers and whooped it up. When I arrived at this orgy I had no idea it was serious. I walked in and everybody was doing everybody else like mad. I was absolutely terrified out of my mind. I found it all terribly shocking, everything looked ugly so I just turned and ran. The last thing I heard as I ran down the road was a man saying, 'Come on — be a sport'. If that's the sporting life — I'll stay away from it.

When I was younger, men made me feel very insecure — and my insecurity made me very eager to please them. I was an only child and I could never understand men properly — never —

148

(now I have given up trying). I always found them very complex – very difficult. And I was very straight forward – couldn't understand deviousness of any kind. So I was never very clever in love. I am a lot more secure now – you become secure when you have been loved as well as I have.

But I can still remember all the times I loved desperately and gave everything. My mother always used to say, 'You must never show a man how much you love him.' Now I realise she was right. If you don't give your all – if you remain your own person – a man will always want to have that inner secret person who belongs to you – the one you won't give. Men search after the soul of a woman – and when a woman is very young – they usually get it. But as you get older – you gather a bit more of yourself together and you lock it in a little room. In your heart you say, 'Yes – you can have *that* bit – because I love you – but you can't have this bit because I want to protect my vulnerable spots.' Because you have been hurt too many times before you build a great wall to protect your vulnerability and so men know they can't get in. If you say to a man, 'I'll give you sex but you can't have love' he hates that. If you tell him he can have love he also wants sex. They want everything – they are not satisfied until they have won the end game!

I never, ever faked with my husband and I have always a lady who liked challenge, excitement, adventure – and if you have those qualities, you are interested in and excited about the person you are in bed with. If a woman asked for my advice on how to be good I'd tell her to be natural – but to use a little artifice now and again.

I have never, ever faked with my husband and I have never counted cracks in the ceiling with anyone else before I was married. But if you do have to fake – my advice as an actress is 'Get into the part because then you will probably become interested halfway through so it will usually end happily'. Ideally you should be able to level with your fella and say, 'Oh darling – I feel like a dishrag tonight.' Faking is really a waste of time – I am a very basic, truthful, down to earth person so it is against my nature to do it.

I would also advise a woman who wants to be good to remember the threes Ts: titillation, technique and tenderness. Titillation starts with the game you play before you go to bed. That

used to be much more exciting than it is nowadays. Today it is
just question and answer. Any man who just said, 'Will you go to
bed with me?' would be out — because he didn't know how to
play the game. The excitement of the chase is often non-existent
today. It used to be such a beautiful, clever, subtle, lovely game;
your hands touched by accident — the hints — the sentences —
the unspoken signal — the purple flash — any question except,
'Will you go to bed with me?' — never that one.

Titillation is also mystery. I don't mean you should go to bed
in a red flannel nightie and say, 'You can see that — but not
this. . .' Mystery is a look in the eye — sometimes you have to
feign mystery with an 'aaha' instead of a yes or no — it's often
difficult for me because I am too straight forward to be really
mysterious. You can also play the game of titillation in bed. You
can pretend it is the first time you have ever been to bed together,
'Ooh — you touched my leg.' You can make the pretence of an
argument — so you lie stiffly in bed as if you're not interested in
the man. He touches you and you pull away. You are using a
little artifice — a little pretence — in order to titillate.

Everyone should have technique. Technique is knowing what
pleases the other person — and you have to find out right at the
beginning. But I think when sex gets to the time of words and
having to say, 'You strike position 2 and I'll strike position 1'
then it is no longer romantic. Sex shouldn't become too technical
— it becomes boring if you've done the same exercises, variations
on a theme, for a thousand and one nights. Technique does go a
long way with a lot of men but there will always come a time
when you have to be more than just technically good in bed —
otherwise the man can always find another woman with a different set of acrobatics to be good in bed for a thousand and
one other nights.

I think both a man and a woman should be receptive to the
other's partner's mood — that's terribly important. It's all a
question of mood and if you do the same routine every time
— sex becomes boring. I do as much as I can to please the
man, without losing my soul or my individuality. If he says,
'I prefer you in suspenders and stockings' — then suspenders and
stockings I'll wear. And if he has any cause for complaint I will
try and put it right. I am not shocked by anything two people do
in bed — providing neither is shocked by anything the other wants.

Once one partner is hurt — the whole picture is shattered and the game is over.

Tenderness matters a great deal in bed. I suppose there are times when a woman likes to be treated like a whore — but only when she is very much loved. But tenderness most of the time. You should both be considerate to one another — that's tenderness, 'Am I hurting you?', 'Are you alright?'. A man should approach you as if you are a fragile doll and what happens after that is nobody's business.

I believe that sex between a man and a woman can be a glorious, beautiful, lecherous, exciting, lustful, gentle, tender adventure. And you should get *involved* — because being uninvolved is a quicker way of dying than any other. You must have passion — you must do everything with passion — people need that, especially in times of tragedy and poverty. Then it suddenly becomes imperative that you are in the middle of life — and sex *is* life. But most of all try a little *love*.

RICHARD BURTON

'What makes a woman G.I.B?' Glamour and beauty have got nothing to do with what makes a woman good in bed. A woman is good if you can talk to her, but more important, if you can laugh with her afterwards.

OLIVER REED

> I discovered Oliver Reed was in Beverly Hills after a friend arranged for a pie to be thrown in Oliver's face. So I phoned Oliver at his hotel, he invited me to dinner — and we did this interview in the bar beforehand. Oliver Reed has always seemed rough, tough and unendingly butch — so I was surprised to find him formal, frostily polite — rather like the head boy of a superior public school.

A woman is good in bed if she accepts the fact that she is going to be fucked. She is the receiver, the vessel, and provided that a woman understands that *she* is going to be penetrated, that she will always be fucked, then a man can have a proper sexual relationship with her.

I am very Victorian in my habits. I have never ever in my life been interested in anything small — in intellect, ideology, sociology, politics, in motor cars, hotel bills, in drinking habits, and certainly not in my ladies. My ladies should be luscious. My ladies should be voluptuous. I like large asses. I prefer large vessles, but not empty vessels. The fashion for thin ladies is only recent. The Pre-Raphaelite, full-hipped ladies of Holman-Hunt were my kind of women. Those used to be the fashionable style of woman, not the wishy-washy, complacent, high-titted society ladies.

Complacency makes a woman bad in bed. I can't tell if a woman is good by just looking at her. But one of the first signs of the woman who might be good is that she has made an effort for the man, that before seeing him she brushes her hair, puts all that shiny stuff on her lips, wears a fresh frock, covers herself with scent, then rushes out to meet him, and pretends that she is a lady.

Age makes a woman good in bed. A boy of seventeen wants to go to bed with a woman of twenty-seven to feel that an older woman is teaching him to make love. A man in his thirties and forties needs the complacency of knowing he can cope with a forty-year-old woman, but at the same time still retains the arrogance of a man who loves to tell himself he has copulated with a woman of under twenty-five.

Romance matters: those mornings with toast and marmalade in bed, when the woman gets back into bed with you and reads the papers. And there are toast crumbs in the bed, and she is very warm, breathing on your shoulder. So you smile and you wake up twenty minutes before the pubs open and she puts on some Mulligatawny soup in the kitchen, and you fall into the bath naked and she falls out of the kitchen naked. Then she puts on a clean frock and you go and play darts in a pub that is full of smoke and you know that you have just left toast crumbs in your bed. That is romance. The romance of going out to an Indian meal, then the movies, and after that, making love for the rest of Sunday. I think *that* is romance that has to be perpetuated through Monday and Tuesday, and I am not literate enough to understand what happens beyond Wednesday.

I don't think a woman would ever refuse something I wanted in bed. But I think that a woman is possibly less good if she *asks* for what she wants in bed. A woman always wants to be dominated in bed, but is afraid to admit it. So she says, 'I want more' and shuffles around the bed, because she has read lots of cheap literature which says that a man is going to ejaculate eight times during the evening if he is James Bond, and now fewer than four times if he is of lesser note. Whereas in reality it will probably, in general, happen once; he will then fall asleep, and later it will happen again twice. A woman should never ever be demanding in bed.

A woman has to understand that in a man's sexual head she is the one who is going to be dominated and abused. A woman *should* be abused, and the woman who is happily abused is a successful lady in bed. I think the woman who is good in bed has to be quite a good slave. She also has to be a willing slave. A willing slave is always warm and humble and submissive and happy to be a slave — and being *that* is what makes a woman good in bed.

DAVID JANSSEN

'What makes a woman G.I.B?' I think it is in the minds of the two people participating.

MARTY FELDMAN

Marty Feldman talked to me in his bungalow at Universal Studios where he was scripting *The Last Remake of Beau Geste*. He sat behind his desk — there was no preliminary chat — Marty just launched into a monologue, which was so rapid that it unnerved me slightly.

I think we are given false expectations about sex, so it never quite measures up to the way sex is in the movies. Sex is the satisfaction of an appetite. It *can* be more than that, but it usually is far less than the media portrays. People get a lot of their ideas about sex from media exaggerations, so now both men and women have some abstract idea of the proper sexual relationship. It's a kind of sexual nirvana which I don't think many people experience.

I found my first sexual experience terribly dissatisfying because I expected it to be cosmic, it was merely enjoyable in the same way as when I first ate houmous. I had heard about it for years,

153

and I happened to like it, but it didn't wake my tastebuds up —
I didn't leap around — it was just very pleasurable.

If I were looking for the perfect women in bed, I would look
for one who tries to please me. Someone who is flexible and will
experiment on an equal basis. That seems to me a reasonable
basis for any relationship, be it sexual or professional, or professionally sexual or sexually professional — whichever way you
come at it, or go at it.

Sex is a collaboration in the truest sense; you both work
together for a common end. After all, my life started with a collaboration between my father and my mother (at least I assume
it was my father; I have no proof). Collaboration runs through life,
and the more you do something together — the more you understand each other's responses and needs — the more you become a
team. Sex is not very different from a soccer team — the end is
different, but the means are the same. Teamwork is understanding
each other's needs and the cause and effect; the effect will be
mutual, the causes will be different.

I knew I could act with Gene Wilder the minute we met.
Chemistry. Had Gene Wilder been an attractive woman, it would
have been a sexual vibration. I can't define it. If you could define
what makes a woman or a man good in bed, then everybody
would do it well, and there would be no mystery in bed.

If two people are inexperienced, they will learn together; if
one person is experienced, he will teach the other; if they're both
very experienced, then they will both get much more fulfillment
and enjoyment out of sex. If you get two skillful performers at
it, they will know how to collaborate. Love can matter in bed, but
I know people who believe they're in love with everyone they
sleep with; perhaps they *are* just for that time.

Sex needn't always be equal, but if not, it is by choice. There
are times when you don't feel like making the going and the woman
makes the going. And there are other times when the man makes
the approach, controls the act, the tempo. The approach doesn't
make any difference, as long as both people are getting maximum
enjoyment out of sex, but you decide everything for yourself.
You don't let anyone else decide for you.

People *do* try and decide what is sexually normal and what is a
deviation. I hate to hear the word 'deviation' because I have yet
to see 'the norm' defined. When I see it defined, then I can discuss

what is abnormal. I don't know what is normal. None of us do, because we don't live in each other's bedrooms. Normal is whatever you enjoy. To quote Hemingway: 'What is moral is what you feel good after.' Any relationship with a predator or a prey is not equal and is therefore not moral or normal.

Sex is two plus two making five, rather than four. Sex is the X ingredient that you can't define, and it's that X ingredient between two people that makes both a man and a woman good in bed. It's all relative. There are no rules. But if there *were* a rule for good sex, it would be: 'Play it by ear,' except, I suppose, the ear is the wrong organ.

ROBERT MITCHUM

'What makes a woman G.I.B?' Proximity.

DAVID HEMMINGS

Although Gayle Hunnicutt, David Hemmings' ex-wife said she thought he would never agree to an interview, I still risked asking David, when I saw him after the Sammy Davis Gala at the London Palladium. He said yes — so we met the next day at the Chelsea Arts Club, in a beer and darts atmosphere, with David in a red polo neck sweater, discussing club committees, very much the local squire. I found that the sixties photographer of *Blow-Up* — all birds and beds — had been replaced by a sober, serious intellectual — the wild boy in his maturity. David's ideas about sex and relationships have obviously been carefully formulated within his three marriages so that he needed very little prompting during the two hours in which we talked. We met again a few months later in David's Mayfair office, after he had asked to read the interview. Surrounded by law books, in the process of casting a film, David still scrutinised the interview carefully, made a a few minor, but thoughtfully considered alterations, then took me to the wine bar downstairs.

Nothing that a woman could or could not do in bed would ever convince me that a relationship should begin or be sustained. I certainly would never judge my women by their performances in bed. I judge my women by the development of the relationship — the development of a joint and several personality. The best thing in the world is to have a woman who really cares — not about herself — nor about you — but about the relationship. A woman who feels that the relationship must be protected at all costs.

I don't judge my women by their beauty. Beauty — particularly in long-term relationships — fades very quickly. One lives with personalities not faces. One lives with friendships — not bodies. And it's harder for a beautiful woman to protect the relationship — because extreme beauty brings with it too many external demands and too many temptations. The man knows his woman is constantly on show — that creates personal pride in him — but he also knows that the only time he will really get the private attention of a really beautiful woman is in the privacy of their own home. The strains on any relationship are greater if the woman is extremely beautiful.

In my personal opinion there are three types of sex. First: friendly sex — which is lovely — rather charming. You've known someone for many years — you happen to meet and you go to bed for friendship's sake. On the very rare occasions I have had friendship sex it has always been an extremely pleasurable experience; warm, reassuring, secure. And I think a woman is always best in bed when she feels secure with her man — and doesn't feel she has to make an effort. She feels secure when a man doesn't make more demands on her than she feels she can cope with.

The second type of sex is a one night stand. That is based on hope rather than good judgement — on convenience and circumstance. Generally both partners are at a loose end and find each other attractive — so — you both go into it (at least, almost certainly, the man) knowing that no long-term continuous relationship will develop. Usually it is a bore; the man will go through his list of particular techniques that he believes have served him well in the past. And the woman will go through her own particular bag of tricks. And in the morning everybody will wake up — lie like mad — say it was wonderful. There is something immensely sad about it.

I have never had a one night stand I would want to repeat. By the same token I *would* repeat every sustained relationship I have had with a woman. I find a long-term affair — the gradual learning, understanding process of a relationship — far preferable to any other kind of sex. I have to have a real personal sense of love and affection before I can make love remotely well.

I am as nervous as any man is nervous on the first night because he wants to be good. I don't have any hang-ups but the first time is terribly difficult. You finally make your escape to the bedroom after coffee — she goes into the bathroom and you frantically get out of your gear — that's horrific. There is so much tension — you've got bra straps all over the place — you can't expect to suddenly click because that's not the way to approach one of the main sections of a relationship.

My approach is to get to know a woman's body before I make love to her. With my wife, Prue, we spent days actually just sleeping together but not making love. We wanted to know each other tremendously well and I think it takes time, days. It's nice to establish a gentle relationship — to get used to one another — with warmth — so both people are at ease. Then gradually, with great affection and, I believe, great romanticism, you have sex.

The first time you make love is very sensitive, very searching, very tentative, a very groping affair. When you start a relationship both partners want to sustain, neither of you wants to do anything sexually that could damage the relationship. So the woman will do her best to make sure she doesn't do anything to turn me off — and I do the same. Both partners tend to be so totally unselfish — to make sure the other partner achieves the maximum enjoyment. You are starting fifteen poles apart because neither partner knows one another and neither partner's being honest — there is a fear of making demands too soon. I believe that both people should go into the first sexual experience being totally selfish. At least you will have no shocks later. Otherwise it is like pretending to be tidy the first few days of a relationship — when you know that in three weeks time you'll be leaving your shirts all over the floor. That is ridiculous — both partners should be as truthful as they can from the start.

However, you can't expect too much too soon. One hopes that over a period of time the personalities of the two people will develop into a relationship. You have to get to know your partner well enough to know what sort of sexual attitudes and experiences they will want, according to their moods; when fantasies can be fulfilled and enjoyed, when sex should take place with great love

157

and tenderness, or toughness and strength and brutality. You have to ring the changes – and you must learn to ring the changes at the right time – that's the trick. It takes a long time to discover.

There is no question that a woman should ask for what she wants in bed. But she has to time her demands according to the mood and conditions. You have to openly discuss what you both require and desire. Sometimes I like to be incredibly passive – other times incredibly active. I sometimes like to be the aggressor and other times I don't. I don't look upon a woman as a sub-missive object – sometimes yes – but not always. A man has to be able to spot moments of insecurity in a woman – to know when to push and when to leave well alone – when to ease back.

A woman sometimes wants to refuse something sexually – that can create problems. If a man wanted desperately to fuck a woman up the arse and she didn't want to, the man would – I suppose – be dissatisfied. That's not an area I know too much about as I don't particularly like it. No one has ever asked me to do it – it's not my particular pleasure.

I don't really believe that there is such a thing as the woman who is bad in bed. I've had bad sexual experiences – but that's always been my fault and not the fault of the woman. Or let me say that I consider myself responsible. I had a wonderful, tremen-dously warm and beautiful relationship with a very well known lady. It was a very exciting personal relationship – we were very much in love – but we could never make it in bed. It was a total and absolute sexual failure – although we were desperately in love in every way. Because of the importance of the relationship we could never make it – but you can't say that particular woman was bad in bed.

Being good in bed is not a physical thing – it's not the physical strength of the orgasm that determines whether or not one has had a successful sexual experience. I know of women who don't actually come – but enjoy the total experience of making love. There have been occasions when it has happened to me but I have still enjoyed the sex. I don't think the orgasm is the clue as to whether the woman was good or not. There are some women who have sixteen orgasms in fifteen minutes and there are others who need one and a quarter hours to make it. You obviously have to treat them differently. You don't go banging away at a woman who takes one and a half hours to come – you have to use different techniques. I personally would not feel I had had a full physical experience unless I felt I had satisfied the woman. Although there are times when a woman says, 'I am just not going to make it tonight.' I don't mind – in any case I don't award myself medals at any time. I don't consider myself to be a stud by any means, shape or form. But I love sex and I love it to be a fulfilling experience. And I don't think you can gauge a fulfilling experience by whether or not the woman had an orgasm.

It's a shame if a woman has to fake – she shouldn't have to. She should discuss it and say, 'In order to orgasm I need X.' If the woman fakes for any length of time – then the man will become convinced that what he's doing is terrific. If one day he does drive the woman to distraction and she finally says, 'I don't really like the way you do it' then the relationship will be terribly damaged. If the sex is not selfish it will ultimately lead to dissatisfaction.

I find that in every relationship there is a moment in time that exemplifies the truly memorable sexual experience. One night – one moment – in a field – in a car – when you don't have to say, 'My God that was terrific.' It just happened to be the sum total of one's entire sexual experience with that person. All of one's subsequent sexual experiences and all the subsequent ways one makes love with that woman will be designed to repeat that memorable moment. I can remember the specific moment like that with my wife.

Prue is extremely good in bed. Most of all because we know each other extremely well – and the most important thing in a marital relationship is total and absolute 100 percent friendship – it has taken me a long time to discover that. I believe more than anything else in having the knowledge that you have a genuine friend – someone who really cares about you and that you care about. Consequently the sexual experience one shares together as a result of that friendship and knowledge are marvellous. If you're friends with someone and your long-term relationship is very, very secure I don't think you can find a sexual alternative that will match it. If you are shrewd enough to remember that you have a really well sustained, genuine friendship with someone and if you forget body, face, everything except truth and friendship and love – there is very little chance you will ever find a better sexual experience in an across-a-crowded-room-fuck than you could have making it at home with your woman.

GEORGE PEPPARD

'What makes a woman G.I.B?' I suppose it's the way she feels about men.

GLENDA JACKSON

> Glenda Jackson did this interview in her dressing room at the Old Vic in London while she was putting her hair into curlers before a performance of *The White Devil*. She had obviously considered the subject carefully, was incredibly articulate, yet never once faltered with a single curler.

I have always resented the phrase 'good in bed'. I have heard men use it — although I must admit that I have never considered it in relation to myself. I take umbrage at it because the concept is part of the myth of a woman being evaluated as a human being only on a very specific level, in a very limited area — with the judge, jury, and hangman in that particular assessment being a man.

It is always very difficult to know what men mean when they say a woman is good in bed. I think that a man thinks a woman is good if she tells him *he* is. So more often than not, 'good' to men, I think, means that the woman has said or done something that has flattered their ego. Some men have a fantasy that they are wondrous in bed, and if they feel they are not, they will turn around and say, 'It is your fault.' But men worry much more about their reputations with one another than with women. So I think that the comment is a generality that men make to each other when they boast about their sexual exploits.

Any assessment of good seems to be grossly unfair. It is unwritten that it is possible to be bad in bed if you say someone is good. It also infers that there is something durable and positive in someone who is good — and something diminishing and demeaning in somebody who is bad. But I don't think that is the case or that the judgment should be made at all. People are not born bad or good in bed. Personally speaking, I think sex is terrific — but there are people one knows who don't think it is. That is a programmed response though, something that has happened to them, part of their upbringing and nothing to do with being born good or bad.

When I was at school there seemed to be very little fantasy of the actual sex act or process, because sex was still strictly on the level of how boys looked, of what made them attractive. We were told that to participate was sufficient — to enjoy sex was not necessary. In any case, then the great danger was not whether you were good or whether you were bad; it was whether you got pregnant. We didn't consider being good; there was a certain belief that you would automatically know what to do, and if you didn't, the man would. I don't think it ever occurred to us to wonder what *we* had to do.

I think today we worry far too much. It's part of our particular society at the moment that people think sex is desperately important and are particularly vulnerable about it and about their own abilities in that particular area. I think if you can't laugh at sex, you are in dead *schtuk*; sex is terribly funny if you think about it. If it is taken as a life-and-death situation, then it will be a total disaster. And even then, if it is lousy, then it's lousy and there are reasons other than physical dexterity or imaginativeness or reading the *Kama Sutra*.

You don't buy being good in bed off a shelf. I don't think there is a program you go through with someone which results in what you expected when you first put your penny in the slot. I don't think it's anything that exists outside your whole self; it is not an area you can put on and take off. It is as much part of what you are as a person — like your predilection in food or holidays, clothes or literature. It is an intrinsic part of you and I don't think you can adopt other people's attitudes and practices.

Whether you are good in bed or not can only be evaluated in a moment: how much you experience, how much the other person experiences. And that is not a moment clouded in mystery. You either know or you don't know; it's either working for you or it isn't. But I don't think sex works all the time, and even with people with whom it works for *you* all the time; there are ups and downs within that situation. If you are in a continuing relationship and the sex isn't working over a long period of time, then the two people should work it out together.

I think you can have a good sexual relationship with a total stranger. It has never really happened to me, but I can see no reason why it shouldn't. Just simply a straight physical turn-on by someone you haven't met before. It would probably work if it didn't conflict too strongly with your view of yourself, of your own particular moral strictures. But it's very difficult to separate sex and morality (even though I think they should be separated). In any case, if there is a temporary relationship and the sex doesn't work, each person can go their separate way, equally free to accuse the other person of being bad in bed. Except that that judgment should only be made to someone on the clear understanding that the judgment is based on only *one* experience.

My experience of men is very limited because I was married for a very, very long time. When you go virtually from school to being married, your experience of sex is so totally limited, even to the level of what you like. That is something you will hopefully learn with someone who will teach you well, and I think I was probably very fortunate. If anyone asked me the way to be good in bed, I would tell them: preferably being in bed with a fellow you wanted to be with and who wanted to be with you.

I think it would be quite difficult for the woman to be good for the man, yet not enjoy the sex herself. If that does happen in a very honest relationship, I think the woman has a responsibility to say, 'Look, without wishing to be critical or totally destroy you, you may think that I am having the most wonderful time in the world, but a time arrives when it all stops for me.' That has to be said, otherwise resentment will build up and the relationship will then be destroyed. I would say that to someone, but it is difficult, because men are very sensitive in that area. They are often taught that men are automatically good in bed, and so they sometimes lack the urge to admit that they are *not* automatically so. Therefore, their whole ethos is to preserve that fantasy for themselves, which makes it very difficult for a woman to admit a lack of actual sexual satisfaction.

I think women can be infinitely kinder, gentler, more loving, and more hopeful. They always believe in tomorrow; they don't stay with the situation they are in; they always believe that there will be something better; they are essentially optimistic. Because of that, a woman would probably put up with a relationship that she did not regard as good on a sexual level, that did not give her sexual satisfaction. I am not sure that the same is true of men.

Men do sometimes try to exert pressure to get what they want in bed. I have never been in an actual situation where a man has made me feel sexually inadequate because I didn't do something that he has wanted — where he has tried to exert any pressure on me. In other areas men have tried — like using the old trick, when I am winning an argument, of saying, 'Well, you're too intelligent to be feminine.' I have had that a lot. And always, in all situations, my intelligence has told me the truth of those situations, the facts, whereas my emotions probably pulled me another way. That is a split I have always had and always will have, but I think it depends on your mood as to which you actually observe.

I think men also try to exert sexual pressure by saying, 'If you love me, you would do it.' If that happened, I would say, 'If you can say that to me, you don't actually love me, so what the fuck am I doing with you anyway?' Then the relationship would be over. If I didn't want to do anything sexually, there would be no pressure on earth the man could exert that would make me do it, and I wouldn't give a fuck how much the man said, 'You're no good.' In any case, I don't believe that there's any general definition of 'good in bed' to be made. It is just something that has to be defined by each person for themselves.

GENE WILDER

'What makes a woman G.I.B?' My strongest feeling is that the more things revert to sexual technique or what makes someone good or bad, the more they lead to the destruction of the natural impulses that make a woman good. The very question insults me. Not that it shouldn't be asked, but when it *is* asked, everyone should realise that there is no answer — no ABCD — that makes a woman good in bed.

The strongest force working for sexual pleasure any time I have made love to a woman was when an honest affection existed between that woman and myself. And I am almost incapable of making love with a woman for just a quick bang — as it is called — however beautiful the woman, or however instantaneously the passing fancy took me. If I did that, I know that not only would the experience be unsatisfactory, but also the event would leave me less than I was before. When there is an affection – I don't say that you have to be in love – when the guards are let down, then the desire to touch and hold overcomes the pounding of the heart.

Just as in acting there is no right way to do a scene, there is no right way to make love. With one woman the criteria would be completely different from with another woman, with different factors making them both good. Some women do things in bed that make you say, 'She made me feel good, I hope I made her feel good'. But then with another woman, it doesn't matter at all if the same things were done or left undone.

ZSA ZSA GABOR

Everyone jokes about Zsa Zsa Gabor's diamonds, but the day she invited me to have lunch with her, she wasn't wearing any. Instead – each one of her finger nails was printed in toning pink stripes – she was wearing very little make-up and a white broiderie Anglaise dress with a pink belt. Zsa Zsa lives in Howard Hughes' old house overlooking the Bel Air valley – with a large garden, echoing with the songs of Johnny Cash – Zsa Zsa's favourite singer ('he's very sexy'). She showed me around her house and took me into her dressing room, which is like a department store – with all the clothes covered in plastic, catalogued and hanging in rows. Zsa Zsa went straight to one of these rows – took out an orange and amber nightgown and said, 'Dahlink – this is for you – it matches your hair perfectly' – which it did. Next she took me into her study, presented me with a copy of her autobiography, showed me cushions embroidered by a fan, talked about her ex-husband Jack Ryan, advised me to wear brown eyeshadow and then made the salad for lunch.

I hate anything learned about sex – anything that is not instinctive. Studied sex is terrible. I hate it. My last husband was like that. He studied everything about sex. He went to classes to learn how to make love. I personally think that when two people like each other, then sex comes naturally. But if they don't like each other, then neither of them will be good in bed.

A woman is born sexy. She can't learn to be sexy. I think you're either sexy or you're not, and a really sexy man can recognize a really sexy woman. You can't become sexy, but surely a man whom you love can make you more sexy if you are not. I would never give advice on being good in bed. If anyone wants advice on that, they should go to a professional woman for it. I never ever have to think about being sexy, because I only go to bed with a person I want to go to bed with and whom I like, so of course that will be good. I think that the man is the most important performer in bed — he has to have the upper hand. I am very feminine — I like the man to take over. Then I react.

I only go to bed with a man I'm very attracted to, have a crush on, or I am madly in love with. Sometimes you can find out immediately if you are attracted to a man — sometimes it develops. Some women are much more receptive to men than others because they are born to like men — they are not just sexy, they like being with men. But then there are some women who don't really like men. I am not talking about lesbians. I am talking about women who don't like men as sexual beings.

I don't believe in good or bad in bed. I believe if a woman is in love and sexy, she will be fantastic in bed. A sexy woman is a woman who likes to make love. It has nothing to do with looks. I think you have to please the man first and then automatically you please yourself. I don't think you need to be in love to be good, you have to have a very strong attraction to someone, and if there is that sexual attraction you'll both be good, but a great sexual attraction doesn't happen often between people. I have always attracted men naturally. I never make any special efforts. I like men and I like to sleep with men that I like. Obviously, I am not a cold woman; a man likes a woman who is not cold, and I think that they recognize that in me.

When you are in bed with a man you love or are attracted to, you don't have to talk about what you like — everything comes naturally. The best way to lose a man is to not let him be his natural self. I think in bed the woman has to be natural, and has to really want to be with the man she is in bed with. Then everything comes naturally. But you really have to be in ecstasy, and when a woman is in ecstasy, she can do anything she wants. Ecstasy has not been rare in my life, but when the ecstasy is gone, I am gone, too. I never stay longer than the ecstasy.

165

I also think there should be some jealousy in a relationship, because when jealousy is gone, it becomes a boring, dreary relationship. It is good to understand a man, but you don't want to know everything about him. You want to be a little puzzled about what he is going to do next.

I never faked anything in my life, but if a woman is definitely subdued with a man, he will like it. A tough and bossy woman is only good for a weak man who wants a tough and bossy woman. I always liked men who are stronger than I am, and the moment I encounter a weak man, I scare him to death and he runs from me anyhow. Building up a man's ego makes *him* better in bed. He will also be more appreciative of a woman. A man who is not Mr. Big has to be built up. He becomes better in bed when he is made to feel like Mr. Big.

Men who really *are* Mr. Big don't need that so much — they want honesty. If a man is very successful and intelligent, then that kind of man always wants an honest woman, and of course a woman who turns him on. But however honest one tries to be with Mr. Big, a woman still has to subdue herself even for a man like that. The big catches all married little subdued women. Those kinds of women built a man up so he felt more masculine.

A very successful and famous man, if he is not spoiled, is a wonderful pleasure to be with, but if he is spoiled, the relationship won't last, because then he is much too big a chore for a woman. It's also very difficult for two famous people to have a man — woman relationship. If the woman is as successful as the man, then she always has to underplay her success so that the man will always feel superior. To be the wife or girlfriend of a successful man is also very difficult because every other woman in the world is after him. Famous male sex symbols have some special kind of attraction for women which turns them on — a kind of magnetism. It doesn't mean, though, that everyone of those magnetic, charismatic, exciting, masculine-looking male stars are really sexy. Usually they are not.

If a woman wants special-status men she has to be special, and that's very difficult. One man wants a very simple, nice woman: the other wants a very difficult and mysterious woman — so you have to find out what that particular man wants, and then you have to live up to it.

You have to try and change yourself for every man you're with.

I never did, but a woman should try. You should try to be like the man wants you to be, but that doesn't mean you have to lose your personality, because if you do that, if you lose your personality, you lose what the man fell in love with in the first place. He fell in love with you as you are, so obviously that is what he wants.

I was always honest with men, but you shouldn't always let a man know how much you care about him. He should never be 100 percent sure that you belong to him, and he should always doubt that you love him. Many men get turned off when you tell them how much you care about them. It's a bore not to be able to tell a man how you feel about him, because if you really love him, it's wonderful to tell him so. You can only tell a really mature, intelligent man exactly how you feel about him.

I think a man likes to chase a woman. The big fault of the American woman is that she chases a man. I think that's very bad. I think I kept Rubirosa so much in love with me always when all the women in the world wanted him because I never really was in love with him. I was in love with George Sanders (who was my husband), but Rubirosa was so exciting, I couldn't resist him sexually. There was a terrific sexual attraction between us, and also he was one of the sweetest, dearest persons ever born. I think if I had been like all the other women in Rubirosa's life, madly in love with him, just making an enormous fuss of him and not letting him chase me, I would have lost him. But like this I never lost Rubirosa – he was always in love with me, was never sure of me, and that was right.

George Sanders did the same to me, and I always loved him. I loved George for the simple reason that he knew how much I needed and loved him. George was so difficult and so interesting; he was such an exciting man, so he always had me dangling off his little finger. He was a challenge because he was intelligent, sophisticated, and very aloof, and that excited me so much. Challenges *are* exciting, but you can never feel comfortable with a man you can never really capture. It is good to be with a man who loves you and looks after you and really cares about you, but that is *not* usually the man who doesn't want you – whom you want – who challenges you. And I have found out since that a woman has to have other challenges in life – not just a man.

167

ROGER MOORE

'What makes a woman G.I.B?' Last time I was asked, I rather flippantly said off the top of my head in reply to the question, 'If she doesn't argue'. But giving the matter deeper thought, I firmly believe it is the element of surprise and complete privacy, plus the man. If there is no privacy then there can be no element of surprise.

DUDLEY MOORE

> Dudley Moore talked to me after he and Peter Cooke had appeared in a sketch on the Beverly and Vidal Sassoon TV show in Hollywood. He was very shy, serious and quiet. Soon after we spoke, Dudley married glamorous American actress Tuesday Weld.

Good in bed is a funny definition, because being good in bed is something that you yourself decide and you will enjoy a woman as much as you decide to. It's not that she turns you on, but that you actually allow yourself to be turned on. And a woman will be good with the man that she decides to give herself to – at a time when she is totally self-confident. The woman makes the woman good in bed – she makes herself good by having confidence in herself. Most women are born with confidence but lose it and I think that truest sexual satisfaction is not technique but confidence, it's not a matter of technique or having a big cock.

If a man is confident in himself he will recognise a confident woman. And I think a confident man wouldn't go to bed with an unconfident woman because he would know it wouldn't work – and the woman would be bad. Not from a technical point of view but being unable to give or let herself go – unable to take love or receive it – always feeling disappointed. Sex is a question of being with a person you want to be with, because if you are you will both be good. When you hear people saying 'She's lousy in bed' that just means that she didn't respond to him and that he didn't respond to her.

Sex is really just a matter of the individual being prepared to give and to take. For the man to see what the woman's needs are and for the woman to see what the man's needs are. A lot of men and women fuck like rabbits because they feel it's exciting or they are driven to sex through guilt or the excitement that comes from something forbidden or something new. But in the end it's all bullshit really. It boils down to confidence in yourself which gives you the ability to take and to give. Therefore you make the woman good and the woman makes you good. She doesn't have to be like a car that gives you 'good handling'. . .

ELLIOTT GOULD

'What makes a woman G.I.B?' It's great to talk about this. I like to be handled gently. Being a large individual, I like to be handled as gently as I am expected to handle my mate. You should be able to tell if a woman is good. She has to have clear eyes and two ears. There is no physical type. Experience makes a woman. A woman of experience, just like a man of experience, would be able to listen, and able to direct in bed.

It's great if a woman asks for what she wants in bed. I love a woman who is point blank specific. If a woman can say, 'This is what I want' (we try to want anything − not to need anything and just to be, just to exist) and can be direct and tell you what it is that is necessary for her to begin, or end, that's great. A woman is not less good if she refuses something. Sometimes it is even more enticing if she refuses to go along.

Women worry about being good in bed, and so do men. Not to be understood. If you are misunderstood, you have failed in bed. I really don't see how a woman can be bad in bed if she shows up, but I suppose rigidity *is* bad in bed. The only thing that is *really* bad in bed is illness and sickness − also people thinking that bed is where sex is meant to be, that a bed should be a bedroom, because a bed can also be grass under a tree, on the beach. Basically, the only reason for being in a bed is to sleep.

They made 'Great Expectations' but we, here, have no expectations and we say, 'Don't expect anything other than being together,' and then, wherever it takes you. One important thing is to be understood and to be touched. To be touched so that the two individuals always have their space and know where they begin and where they become part of each other.

Sex is different every time. Sex is different every time for the same two people − people who have a relationship and just want

169

to spend time with one another. Sex should be new every time for the relationship to develop. I feel double values don't work in sex, and that two people have to be able to be one another, which is very stimulating — to be with someone I like, who can be me, and who I can be.

GAYLE HUNNICUTT

Beautiful Texas-born actress Gayle Hunnicutt didn't really want to do an interview but decided to see me anyway. When I arrived at her house in South Kensington she had a bad cold after a weekend sailing near Chichester. Her small son Nolan, who looks just like his father David Hemmings, wanted to sit with us in Gayle's bedroom, but Gayle was very firm so instead Nolan showed me where he had planted a tree in the square opposite. Gayle was very curious about the book, still didn't want to do an interview, but decided to give me her reasons for refusing. She was very serious, composed and extremely dignified — telling me her thoughts on the subject in the form of a monologue. When Gayle talked about having elected to live alone, we stopped the tape and discussed the problems we both confronted as single career women in a 'man's world'.

This is a difficult subject for me to discuss. It is not a subject I delve into, even within myself. I am very lucky — there are other fears in my life which I contend with that perhaps other people don't — but sex happens to be an area in which I am very stable, in which there is no conflict. Sex has always seemed terribly easy and right.

For me, discussing sex is rather like discussing diets. If you have a good metabolism, then eating should be a very natural thing. But if you have a problem, then you discuss diets. I wouldn't want to sit around and discuss why a *soufflé* is good. I just enjoy it. I wouldn't like to discuss it, except with a chef — then you venture into a highly specialised area.

To me one's approach to sex should be very understated, and natural. Very much on wavelengths. Something that happens in a very relaxed, gentle way — not at all premeditated or for conquest. I think it would be very difficult, without working on it,

170

to change someone's approach to sex — unless they were really having a problem.

I am basically monogamous — I think that's in my nature. If I am not emotionally quite deeply involved with someone then he has no part in my love life whatsover. I have very many really genuine platonic relationships. As a career girl, having elected to live alone and deal with the world pretty much as a man does, as well as bringing up a child, I find it very comforting to know that I have some very good male friends. When I *do* get involved with someone — he has to learn to know me well enough to realise that I *am* monogamous — so that if I say, 'I am going to go out to dinner with a friend' I mean just that. But most men are highly suspicious and never believe you at the beginning. Eventually they realise that I am very honest and it's difficult for me to sham.

I can't think of a serious relationship I've had, that hasn't lasted at least two years. When it begins to deteriorate — the first place it begins to go wrong is sex. I turn off like a tap. So everything comes to a grinding halt. I never play power games or any kind of games ever, ever — and I don't want them played with me.

I've had one extremely complicated relationship in my life which I think did involve very deep emotional games. They weren't power games, but were the result of two complex personalities getting involved, trying to work it out, but being unable to work through the maze. But we never played games for the sake of playing games.

I had a very strict upbringing in the South and I don't want to analyse sex. My feelings about analysing it are parallel to my feelings about acting. I rarely talk about acting to other actors. You must have very firm foundations for every character you create — some people like to read about the character, other people don't. Some people need research, other people are spontaneous. I have to be spontaneous because they are both fragile and spontaneous areas and for me too much analyses may cause one to lose the magic, the dream, and the fantasy.

If I ever started to analyse sex or really stopped to think about it, I might become frightened. Then sex would either become ludicrous, or hilarious, or worrying or grotesque, or even frightening.

171

Postscript on Speaking Frankly

Gayle Hunnicutt's interview marks the completion of two year's research on sexual attitudes. At the time of the interview I was, perhaps, too close to the project. So Gayle's personal attitude disturbed me. I had sudden doubts and wondered momentarily if my work would tarnish 'the magic, the dream and the fantasy'. However, when I read psychologist James Hemming's *New Society* article 'Sexual Paperchase' on the effects of 'good in bed' — my original premise was corroborated and I realised once more that 'good in bed' is indeed a valid issue affecting present day relationships between men and women.

As a postscript I spoke to Dr. Hemming about the subject and then showed him this manuscript for his comments;

DR. JAMES HEMMING

25 years ago, women were still visiting psychiatrists because they worried about being too passionate. Now we have come out of the darkness of hundreds of years of prudery and women are at last freer. However, the phrase 'good in bed' is inhibiting to today's woman. 'Good in bed' is an artificial standard which is gradually obtruding from the spate of sexual material of all kinds that has poured over us in recent years. This has created the myth of supersex; the suggestion that sex ought to be superlative at all times.

The media projects standards of sexuality, and women often measure themselves against an assumed absolute standard derived from the plays and films they see, the books they read — and then feel doubtful about whether they are meeting those standards. For example; they read about other women having multiple orgasms and think, 'If I have multiple orgasms, this man will feel I am absolutely splendid — the best possible lover.' Instead they should base their standards on their own sexual experience, their own sexual reality.

The whole idea of 'good in bed' and supersex has created an expectation of perfection which no-one has fully defined. So everyone is chasing a fantasy and the expectation of perfect sexual performance leads to each partner being nervous about whether they are 'good' or not. I think that the formalisation and commercialisation of sex is doing a lot of damage to sexual happiness as both men and women are now terribly afraid that they may be going wrong in terms of their own sexual performance.

We are no longer sure by which rules people are playing the sex game. We are now more free, but we don't know what to do as individuals. The old taboos have gone but I think we need to formulate some new rules by which to play the mating game in the modern world. Personally, I think that these rules should be ordinary humane rules of considering one another, of not cheating or lying or exploiting, of being honest.

I am generalising — but I think that the current vogue is for the woman to play an active part in bed. I think passivity, like virginity, is out of date. I don't mean that the woman should be aggressive — but that she is no longer the submissive little woman whom men feel they can devour and dominate with their 'masculine superiority'. I think today's ideal sexual woman is active, starts by not being too cold, doesn't need to be wooed too hard, is fairly approachable — so that the man doesn't have to work on her too much. She moves into the sexual scene — helps the man, and responds to him. And if she 'comes', as they say, then the man feels he has been a great guy. If she doesn't on any particular occasion then nobody feels a flop.

I believe there should be gentle communication in bed — by gesture or touch — and the expressing of pleasure when you feel it. Little verbal promptings help — such as 'that's lovely' or 'not quite so hard'. However, bed is an emotional, not a linguistic area, and I think that sexual problems and desires should be discussed *before* bed. In an area as sensitive as sex you should feel your way along in general terms — asking what sort of sexual experience the other person likes in bed. Then the partner will usually respond by asking in return.

Unfortunately people often dislike discussing what they want in bed, believing it will show that they are 'no good'. Of course — you can go to bed, chance it, and let things follow on. But it seems very curious to me that a man and a woman often go to bed with one another without knowing anything about each other's expectations. Sex is about the only situation in which we do this. If two people plan to go on a holiday together — they discuss what they like first; 'Do you like the mountains or the sea — travelling around or staying put?" — and so forth.

A woman should tell a man beforehand if she doesn't like something in bed – but at the same time she should also add, 'What I really do like is this.' So that she builds – giving something back if she has taken something else away. But the moment a man starts using blackmail along the lines of, 'If you don't like this, or respond like that – you are no good.' – he is being unfair and cruel. To put a person down sexually is one of the cruellest things we can do to one another because it really hits at the basic confidence of people.

There are women who are bad in bed. However, I no longer say that these conditions are incurable because in my time I've seen the most extraordinary transformations. Some women *are* inhibited – afraid of their feelings, afraid of their sexuality, have still got too many guilts lurking around, either from their parents or others and can't move into sexual experiences and let go. The right sort of help and the right sort of partner can rescue these women from their apprehensions and permit their repressed sexual capacities to flower.

I personally think that 'good in bed' is a partnership – not a person. It's not what you do – it's how you relate. And that's very much a here and now thing of being sensitive to the person you are in bed with – responding to them very much in the here and now. I think that the partner who is 'good' is warm, passionate, relaxed, establishes a gentle sort of communication and helps the other person. Then if one partner is feeling very passionate the other will respond by being very passionate or if the other person is feeling quietly loving, then the other will respond by being quietly loving. Also each partner will be tender and appreciative, after the sex is over. In good loving the greatest feeling of togetherness comes with the closeness of the aftermath.

Every sexual experience is really an exploration of the other partner and should be highly reciprocal. People wear masks, and behind each mask is a much frailer, a much more needful, much more insecure person. And the partner who is 'good' takes off their mask and says, 'Here I am – a needful human being – ready to love you'.

The value of this book is that it reflects the human reality behind the sex manuals, so that instead of supersex, we have human sex. It gets away from all formulas, humanising that great destructive force in sexual emancipation; the depersonalisation of sex. The people interviewed were asked about being good in bed, and they responded as human beings, showing the great variety, the unexpectedness, the varied approaches and desires of people.

If all those appealed to had said the same thing, had given *the* formula for being good in bed, then the ordinary person, falling short of that formula would have felt diminished.

I would hope that the book will make everyone feel better, by removing the feeling, 'I am no good in bed because I don't meet the absolute' because I think the book has abolished the absolute by showing the infinite variety of the possible.

It shows that being good isn't one thing, but a whole range of things; therefore we can all join in, because each individual may be good in bed in his or her own way.

I hope the book will help people, reassure them, giving them confidence in their own sexual capacities and in their potentiality for greater sexual happiness.